EX LIBRIS

Bob Brooks

WHO'S WHO
IN THE BIBLE
AN A B C CROSS REFERENCE OF
NAMES OF PEOPLE IN THE BIBLE

Compiled and Edited by
Rev. ALBERT E. SIMS
and
Rev. GEORGE DENT

THE PHILOSOPHICAL LIBRARY
New York

Distributed by
Castle Books
a division of Book Sales Inc.
110 Enterprise Avenue
P.O. Box 2334
Secaucus, N.J. 07094-0934

Manufactured in the United
States of America

85 86 87   9 8 7 6

ISBN 8022-1577-7

PRONUNCIATION OF BIBLICAL NAMES

No authoritative system of pronunciation of Biblical names has been reached. We have to be content with a middle course, avoiding on the one hand a pedantic precision which would offend the ear, and on the other a popular carelessness that often hides the true significance of the name. The following hints may be of service to the average reader :

VOWELS AND DIPHTHONGS.—For general purposes *a* has the same sound as in b*a*, or, if short, as in b*a*ttle ; *e* as in m*e*te or m*e*t, accordingly as it is long or short ; *i* when long may be as in f*i*ne, or as in mach*i*ne; when short, as in b*e*t ; *o* is very much the same as in English ; *u* is used variously, as in t*u*ne, pr*u*de, f*u*n, or t*u*rner.

CONSONANTS.—*G* is usually pronounced hard before a, e, i, as in *g*arment, *G*erizim, *G*ideon ; *ch* is usually hard as in *Ch*ebar, Ario*ch*, but it feels the influence of English in Ra*ch*el and *Ch*erub ; c, s, and t=*zh* or *sh* before *ai* and *iu* cp. Asia, Cappadocia, etc.

The following typical names are given that they may serve as a general guide :

AA'-ron	Al-phæ'us	Bak-buk-i'ah
A-bed'nego	A-mit'täi	Bar-je'sus
A-bi'a	Am'mi-el	Bar-jo'na
A-bi'a-thar	Am'ra-phel	Bar'-sa-bas
A'bi-el	An-a-ni'ah	Bar-ti-mæ'us
A-bi-e'zer	An-dro-ni'cus	Bar-zill'a-i
A-bi'hu	A'ni-am	Bath'she-ba
A-bi'jam	An'ti-pas	Be-a-li'ah
A-bim'-elech	Ap'phi-a (=Affia)	Be-el'ze-bub
A-bi'ram	Ar-chip'pus	Be'li-al
A'bra-ham	Ar-e'tas	Bel-shaz'zar
Ab'sa-lom	Ar'te-mas	Bel-te-shaz'zar
Æne'-as	As-a-i'ah	Ben'ha-dad
Ag'a-bus	As'e-nath	Ben'ja-min
A-ha-zi'ah	Ash'ke-naz	Ben-zo'heth
A-hi'jah	As'ri-el	Ber'a-chah
A-him'e-lech	Ath-a-li'ah	Ber-ni'ce
A-hi'shar	Az-a-ni'ah	Be-thu'el
A-i'jah	A-zu'bah	Be-zal'e-el
Al-mo'dad	Ba'al-i	Big'va-i

3

Bo-a-ner′ges

Ca-i′-a-phas
 (*Cay-i-a-fas*)
Can′da-ce
Che-dor′la-o′mer
Cle′o-phas

Dan′i-el
Deb′o-rah
Del′i-lah
Di-ot′re-phes

E′bed-me′lech
El′a-dah
El′da-ah
E′le-ad
El-e-a′zar
El-ha-nan
E-li′ab
E-li′a-saph
E-li′a-shib
E′li-el
E-li-e′zer
E-li′hu
El′i-ka
E-lim′e-lech
E-li′phaz
E-lish′a-ma
E-lish′a-phat
E-lish′e-ba
E-li′ud
E-liz′a-phan
El′mo-dam
El′na-than
El′pa-al
Elu′za-i
El′y-mas
Ep′a-phras
E-paph-ro-di′-tus
E′phra-im
E′sar-had′don
Esh-tem′o-a
Eth′ba-al
Eu-bu′lus
Eu-ni′ce
Eu-o′di-as

Ga′bri-el
Gad-a-renes

Gad′di-el
Ga′i-us (*Ga-yus*)
Gam′ma-dims
Ged-a-li′ah
Ge-ha′zi
Ge-mal′li
Gem-a-ri′ah
Gid-dal′ti
Gid′e-on
Gil′a-läi
Go-li′ath

Ha-a-hash′ta-ri
Ha-ba′iah
Hab′ak-kuk
Hach-a-li′ah
Hach′mo-ni
Had-ad-e′zer
Ham-med′a-tha
Ham-mol′e-keth
Han′a-ni
Han-a-ni′ah
Ha-ru′maph
Hash-a-bi′ah
Hash-bad′a-na
Ha-su′pha
Ha′za-el
Hez-e-ki′ah
Hod-a-vi′ah
Ho-se′a (*Ho-ze′a*)
Ho-she′a
Hy-men-æ′us

Ib-nei′ah
Ich′a-bod
Im-man′u-el
I-ri′jah
I-sai′iah
Is-car′i-ot
Ish′bo-sheth
Ish′ma-el
Ish-ma-i′ah
Is-ma-chi′-ah
Is′ra-el
Is′sa-char
Ith′a-mar
It′ta-i

Ja′a-kan
Ja-ak′o-bah

Ja′i-rus
Ja-ro′ah
Jath′ni-el
Je-da′iah
Jed-e-di′ah
Jeh-dei′ah
Je-ho′a-haz
Je-ho′ash
Je-hoi′a-da
Je-hon′a-dab
Je-ho′ram
Je-ho′vah
Je-hu′di
Jem′i-ma
Je-mu′el
Je-phun′neh
Jer-e-mi′ah
Je-ri′ah
Je-ri′jah
Jer-o-bo′am
Je-rub′ba-el
Jesh′u-a
Jez-a-ni′ah
Jez′e-bel
Jo-an′na
Jon′a-than
Jo′ri-ah
Josh′a-phat
Josh′u-a
Jo-si′ah

Kad′mi-el
Ke-mu′el
Ke-zi′a
Kol-a-i′ah
Kush-ai′ah

La′a-dah
Laz′a-rus
Lem′u-el

Ma′a-cah
Ma-a-sei′ah
Ma-a-zi′ah
Mach-na-de′bai
Ma-ha′zi-oth
Mal-chi′ah
Mal-chi′jah
Ma-nas′seh
Ma-no′ah

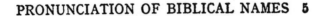
Mat-ta-ni'ah
Mat'thi'as
Mat-ti-thi'ah
Me-het'a-bel
Me-hu'ja-el
Mel-chiz'e-dek
Men'a-hem
Me-phib'o-sheth
Mer'a-ri
Mesh-el-e-mi'ah
Me-thu'selah
Mir'i-am
Mish'a-el

Na'a-mah
Na'a-rai
Nah'bi
Na'o-mi
Na-than'a-el
Ne-a-ri'ah
Neb-u-chad-nez'zar
Neb-u-zar'-a-dan
Ne-he-mi'ah
Ne-mu'el
Nic-o-de'mus
Nic'o-las
No-a-di'ah

Ob-a-di'ah
O-nes'i-mus
On-e-siph'o-rus

Par'me-nas
Pat'ro-bas
Pek-a-hi'ah
Pel-a-ti'ah
Pe-ul'thäi

Pha'ra-oh (Fa'ro)
Phi-le'mon
Phi-le'tus
Phi-lol'o-gus
Phin'e-has
Phy-gel'lus
Poch'e-reth
Pot'i-phar
Po-tiph'e-ra
Proch'o-rus

Quar'tus
Qui-rin'i-us

Rab-sha-keh
Ra-mi'ah
Re-el-äi'ah
Re-ho-bo'am
Rem-a-li'ah
Reph-a-i'ah
Ro-man-ti-e'zer

Sab'te-cha
Sa-lo'me
Sap-phi'ra
Sce'va (Se'va)
Sem-a-chi'ah
Sen-nach'e-rib
Shash'a-i
She-ar-ja'shub
Shec-a-ni'ah
Shel-e-mi'ah
She-mu'el
Shesh-baz'zar
Shim'e-i
Sis'e-ra
Sop'a-ter
Steph'a-nas

Ta'be-el
Tab'ri-mon
Tah'pe-nes
Tan'hu-meth
Tat'na-i
Teb-a-li'ah
Te-hin'nah
Ter-tul'lus
Thad-dæ'us
The-oph'i-lus
Tir'ha-nah
Tir-sha-tha
To-bi'ah
To-bi'jah
To-gar'mah
Troph'i-mus
Tych'i-cus
Ty-ran-nus

U'ri-el
Uz-zi'ah
Uz-zi'el

Va-ni'ah
Voph'si

Za'a-van
Zac-chæ'us
Zach-a-ri'ah
Zeb'e-dee
Zech-a-ri'ah
Ze-mi'ra
Zeph-a-ni'ah
Ze-ru'ah
Ze-rub'ba-bel
Zip-po'rah
Zu-ri-shad'dai

GENERAL NOTES

The references are to the Authorised Version (i.e. the one in general use), unless otherwise indicated. RV. = Revised Version.

" f." placed after a reference means the following verse; " ff." means the following verses.

Large Roman numerals indicate the number of the book where there are more than one. Small Roman numerals indicate the chapter, and Arabic figures the verse or verses.

Where several persons are grouped under the same name, the sequence is generally indicated by Arabic figures.

Names of Biblical book references are abbreviated as follows :
Gen. = Genesis.
Ex. = Exodus.
Lev. = Leviticus.
Num. = Numbers.
Deut. = Deuteronomy.
Josh. = Joshua.
Judg. = Judges.
Ruth = Ruth.
I Sam. = I Samuel.
II Sam. = II Samuel.
I Kings = I Kings.
II Kings = II Kings.
I Chron. = I Chronicles.
II Chron. = II Chronicles.
Ezra = Ezra.
Neh. = Nehemiah.
Esther = Esther.
Job = Job.
Psalms = Psalms.
Prov. = Proverbs.
Eccles. = Ecclesiastes.
Song of S. = Song of Solomon.
Isaiah = Isaiah.
Jer. = Jeremiah.
Lam. = Lamentations.
Ezek. = Ezekiel.
Dan. = Daniel.
Hos. = Hosea.
Joel = Joel.
Amos = Amos.
Obad. = Obadiah.
Jonah = Jonah.

Micah = Micah.
Nahum = Nahum.
Hab. = Habakkuk.
Zeph. = Zephaniah.
Hag. = Haggai.
Zech. = Zechariah
Mal. = Malachi.

Matt. = Matthew.
Mark = Mark.
Luke = Luke.
John = John.
Acts = Acts.
Rom. = Romans.
I Cor. = I Corinthians.
II Cor. = II Corinthians.
Gal. = Galatians.
Ephes. = Ephesians.
Phil. = Philippians.
Col. = Colossians.
I Thess. = I Thessalonians.
II Thess. = II Thessalonians.
I Tim. = I Timothy.
II Tim. = II Timothy.
Titus = Titus.
Philemon = Philemon.
Heb. = Hebrews.
James = James.
I Pet. = I Peter.
II Pet. = II Peter.
I John = I John.
II John = II John.
III John = III John.
Jude = Jude.
Rev. = Revelation.

6

PREFACE

THOUGH perhaps any such statement is somewhat superfluous, the compilers deem it well to say that this Biblical Who's Who has been treated from a popular rather than a critical standpoint—that it is intended for the general reader rather than for the student.

Owing to limitations of space, only those personalities likely to have general appeal have been presented with any fulness of detail, yet no name of importance has been omitted ; textual references have been kept to the minimum, for the sake of brevity and conciseness—the intelligent use of a good Reference Bible will enable a reader to trace any personality through all textual passages.

In discharging their task the compilers have consulted the best modern authorities, and to these sources they frankly acknowledge their indebtedness and express the hope that their work will form a useful compendium of information presented in popular style, which will enable anyone to understand at a glance " Who's Who " in the Bible.

ALBERT E. SIMS
GEORGE DENT

THE GENERATIONS OF JESUS

According to Matthew

Abraham	Obed	Achaz	Sadoc
Isaac	Jesse	Ezekias	Achim
Jacob	David	Manasses	Eliud
Judas	Solomon	Amon	Eleazar
Phares	Roboam	Josias	Matthan
Esrom	Abia	Jechonias	Jacob
Aram	Asa	Salathiel	Joseph
Aminadab	Josaphat	Zorobabel	CHRIST
Naasson	Joram	Abiud	
Salmon	Ozias	Eliakim	
Booz	Joatham	Azor	

According to Luke (Luke's genealogy is here inverted in order to provide a parallel table so as to facilitate comparison between the two lists).

Adam	Abraham	Joseph	Semei
Seth	Isaac	Juda	Mattathias
Enos	Jacob	Simeon	Maath
Cainan	Juda	Levi	Nagge
Maleleel	Phares	Matthat	Esli
Jared	Esrom	Jorim	Naum
Enoch	Aram	Eliezer	Amos
Mathusala	Aminadab	Jose	Mattathias
Lamech	Naasson	Er	Joseph
Noe	Salmon	Elmodam	Janna
Sem	Booz	Cosam	Melchi
Arphaxad	Obed	Addi	Levi
Cainan	Jesse	Melchi	Matthat
Sala	David	Neri	Heli
Heber	Nathan	Salathiel	Joseph
Phalec	Mattatha	Zorobabel	JESUS
Ragau	Menan	Rhesa	
Saruch	Melea	Joanna	
Nachor	Eliakim	Juda	
Thara	Jonan	Joseph	

THE KINGS OF JUDAH AND ISRAEL

WITH APPROXIMATE DATES

B.C.		
1048	SAUL	
1009	DAVID	
969	SOLOMON	

B.C.	JUDAH	ISRAEL
940	Rehoboam	Jeroboam
920	Asa	
918		Nadab
915		Baasha
891		Elah
888		Zimri, Omri
876		Ahab
874	Jehoshaphat	
853		Ahaziah
852		Joram
849	Jehoram	
844	Ahaziah	
842	Athaliah	Jehu
836	Joash	
814		Jehoahaz
798		Joash
797	Amaziah	
783		Jeroboam II
778	Uzziah	
743	(Azariah)	Zechariah (6 months)
		Shallum (1 month)
		Menahem
740	Jotham	
738		
737		Pekahiah
736	Ahaz	Pekah
730		Hoshea
727	Hezekiah	
695	Manasseh	
641	Ammon	
639	Josiah	
608	Jehoahaz	
	Jehoiakim	
	Jehoiakin	
597	Zedekiah-	
	Captivity.	

HOW TO USE THE BOOK

With the aid of an ordinary Reference Bible fuller particulars of any person mentioned may easily be obtained.

For instance, *Caiaphas* has the *reference* John xi. 49-53 given. If we turn up this passage and look up the *marginal references*, we learn :

> *Luke iii.* 2. Annas and Caiaphas were high priests when the word of God came to John (the Baptist) in the wilderness.

> *John xviii.* 14. " Now Caiaphas was he, which gave council to the Jews, that it was expedient that one man should die for the people."

> *Acts iv.* 6. That Caiaphas was one of those before whom Peter and the other Apostles appeared soon after Pentecost.

In this way we can, from the start given in this book, build up the full story of Caiaphas as recorded in the New Testament.

AARON—elder brother of Moses, evidently born before Pharaoh's infanticide edict (Ex. vi. 16 f.). Was divinely appointed spokesman of Moses when he sought from Pharaoh the liberation of the Israelites. With Ur, he supported Moses' hands in prayer during Joshua's battle with Amalek (Ex. xvii. 12). He acquiesced in calf-worship whilst Moses was in the Mount with God (Ex. xxxii. 1-29). When Korah led a rebellion against him and Moses, Aaron's rod was made to bud (Num. xvii. 1-13). Subsequently by divine appointment he was stripped of his robes, and these were transferred to his son, Eliezar (Num. xx. 22 f.). He was feebler in character than his illustrious brother Moses.

ABAGTHA—one of Ahasuerus' seven chamberlains (Esther i. 10).

ABDI—1. Father of Kishi (I Chron. vi. 44). 2. Son of Elam (Ezra x. 26).

ABEDNEGO—one of Daniel's three companions (Dan. i. 7). (*see* Azariah).

ABEL—second son of Adam. A shepherd. Offered "a more excellent sacrifice" than Cain (Gen. iv. 1-16). Was murdered by Cain through envy.

ABI—mother of King Hezekiah (II Kings xviii. 2).

A B I A H—1. Grandson of Benjamin (I Chron. vii. 8). 2. Second son of Samuel (I Sam. viii. 2). 3. Wife of Hezron (I Chron. ii. 24). *Equivalent*, Abijah.

ABIATHAR—a priest. On the slaughter of Doeg he escaped and went over to David (I Sam. xxii. 20-23). Appears to have shared the high priesthood with Zadok. Subsequently joined Adonijah, and was ejected from his high priesthood.

ABIDAH—a son of Midian (Gen. xxv. 4).

ABIEL—1. Father of Kish and of Ner (I Sam. ix. 1 ; xiv. 51). 2. One of David's " mighty men," also called Abialbon (I Chron. xi. 32).

ABIEZER—1. A descendant of Manasseh (Josh. xvii. 1, 2). 2. One of David's " mighty men " (II Sam. xxiii. 27).

ABIGAIL—1. Wife of Nabal, and afterwards of David (I Sam. xxv. 3). 2. David's second sister (II Sam. xvii. 25).

ABIHAIL—1. Wife of Rehoboam (II. Chron. xi. 18).

11

2. Wife of Abishur (I Chron. ii. 29).

ABIHU—second son of Aaron (Ex. vi. 23).

ABIHUD—grandson of Benjamin (I Chron. viii. 3).

ABIJAM—son and successor of Rehoboam. Followed in his father's sin. Gained a great, though fruitless, victory over Jeroboam. Was succeeded by his son Asa (I Kings xv. 1).

ABIMAEL—son of Joktan. Founded a famous nomad Arab tribe near Mecca (Gen. x. 28).

ABIMELECH—1. King of Gerar, with whom Abraham had dealings (Gen. xx. 3). 2. Son of Gideon, who massacred many of his kindred (Judg. ix. 1-57). 3. A priest; son of Abiathar (I Chron. xviii. 16).

ABINADAB—1. A Kirjath-jearimite who harboured the ark (I Sam. vii. 1-2). 2. Elder brother of King David (I Sam. xvi. 8). 3. Son of Saul, killed, like his father, at Gilboa (I Sam. xxxi. 2).

ABINOAM—father of Barak (Judg. iv. 6).

ABIRAM—1. Brother of Dathan, with whom he joined in rebellion against Moses (Num. xvi. 1). 2. Firstborn of Hiel. Died as punishment when his father began to rebuild Jericho (I Kings xvi. 34).

ABRAHAM—eldest son of Terah. Born at Ur (Chaldea); removed with his father to Haran (Mesopotamia), and afterwards followed God's leading in going to Palestine, the whole of the territory of which was promised to him for an inheritance; sojourned in the Valley of Shechem, and built an altar at Bethel (House of God). Famine caused him to flee to Egypt. Here he practised deception in defence of his wife, and was rebuked by the Egyptian king. He returned to Palestine with Lot, his nephew. Each found his possessions so greatly increased that they decided to separate. Lot chose the Cities of the Plain. Abraham afterwards rescued him from the confederacy of "five kings" against four. On his return from the battle Abraham offered tithes to Melchizedek. Feeling disappointed that his wife bore him no heir, he gained a son (Ishmael) through Hagar, though afterwards Sarah bore Isaac to him. He sought deliverance for Sodom (or, rather, for Lot and his family), and this was brought about so far as Lot's family was concerned, though the evil cities were overthrown. A supreme test faced him when he felt called upon to sacrifice Isaac, but he was saved from this at the eleventh hour after his willingness to obey at all costs had been proved. His wife Sarah died and was buried in the Cave of Machpelah. He sent his servant to Mesopotamia to seek a wife for Isaac. He died at a great age. He stands out as a pioneer soul at the dawn of recognised history. Members of his race have looked to him in all generations as the Father of the Faithful and the founder of their people. His outstanding characteristic was an intense faith in God, which guided him, with one or two slips, through all his conduct (Gen. xii. 1, *onward*).

ABSALOM—third son of David ; beautiful in appearance ; his father's favourite, against whom he rebelled and was exiled. After five years had elapsed his father allowed him to return. He won the hearts of the people from David and sought to seize the throne. After much scheming war broke out, but David's veterans gained the victory. Absalom, riding furiously away, was caught by his hair in an oak and, his horse rushing on, he was left suspended till Joab came and thrust three darts through his heart, thus despatching the unfortunate rebel. When David heard the news he gave way to excessive grief (II Sam. xviii. 1, etc.). Psalms xlii. and xliii. are thought to refer to Absalom's rebellion.

ACHAICUS—a Christian who came to see Paul (I Cor. xvi. 17).

ACHAN—a son of Carmi. Took the " accursed thing" at the siege of Jericho by Joshua, thus occasioning the defeat at Ai. Was stoned to death in the Valley of Achor (Josh. vii. 16 f.).

ADAH—1. One of Lamech's wives (Gen. iv. 19-21). 2. One of Esau's wives (Gen. xxxvi. 2-4).

ADAIAH—1. Josiah's mother (II Kings xxii. 1). 2. A Levite, son of Ethan (I Chron. vi. 41-42). 3. A priest, son of Jeroham (I Chron. ix. 12). 4. A Benjamite (I Chron. viii. 21). 5. A son of Bani (Ezra x. 29). 6. A son of Joiarib (Neh. xi. 5). 7. The father of Maaseiah (II Chron. xxiii. 1).

ADALIA—one of Haman's ten sons (Esther ix. 8).

ADAM—the name of the first man of the race (according to the Creation story of *Genesis*) who was made in the image of the Divine and was placed in a holy and happy estate, but who by his disobedience wilfully broke covenant with his Maker and thereby fell from favour and grace (Gen. ii. ff.).

The New Testament regards Adam as the father of the whole human race —so vitally identified with all men, that he by the hereditary transmission of his guilt involved all his posterity in his misery (Romans v.), though divine judgment is so set forth that it does not become operative in a *personal* sense until the individual will, by its free volitions, makes Adam's sin its own.

The teaching of St. Paul (I Cor. xv. etc.) establishes a close parallelism between Adam and Christ (the second Adam)—the first sensuous, the second heavenly—and insists on the *oneness* of mankind in the physical union with Adam (and thereby involved in the consequences of his fall) and our spiritual union with Christ (who is the Saviour and Redeemer of all who truly believe in Him).

ADBEEL—a son of Ishmael (Gen. xxv. 13).

ADER—a Benjamite, son of Elpaal (I Chron. viii. 15).

ADRIEL—husband of Saul's daughter Merab (I Sam. xviii. 19).

ÆNEAS—a paralytic healed by Peter (Acts ix. 32 f.).

AGABUS—a prophet who predicted a great famine (Acts xi. 28) ; he also pictorially predicted Paul's captivity (Acts xxi. 10).

AGAG—1. A king of Amalek (Num. xxiv. 7).   2. A king of Amalek slain by Samuel after having been spared by Saul (I Sam. xv. 9).

AGEE—one of David's mighty men (II Sam. xxiii. 11).

AGRIPPA I—*equivalent*, " Herod the King " (Acts xii, 1 ff). Born about 10 B.C. ; son of Aristobulus and Bernice ; is described as " magnanimous, reckless, extravagant " ; given to bribery. Had to leave Rome, and at one time contemplated suicide. Imprisoned, but released

by Caligula and succeeded to the tetrarchies of Philip and Lysanias, and was entitled " king." He cultivated friendship with the Jews.   He lived a life of strict Pharisaism.   Persecuted the Christian Church, slaying James and imprisoning Peter.   Was greeted as a god at the public games ; died a painful death, being eaten of worms.   This was regarded as punishment for his blasphemy. (*See* Herod.)

AGRIPPA II—son of Agrippa and Cypros.   On the death of his uncle, Herod of Chalcis, he succeeded to the tetrarchy, with the oversight of the temple. Later he gave up Chalcis and took over the tetrarchies of Philip and Lysanias.   Was interested in Jewish questions.   Paul recognised his expert knowledge when summoned before Agrippa's presence.   Agrippa then confessed, either in jest or earnest, that he was " almost persuaded to be a Christian " (Acts xxvi. 28).

AGUR—son of Jakeh (Prov. xxx. 1).

AHAB—1. Son and successor of Omri.   Married the idolatrous Jezebel, and came under her evil influence.   Sought to slay Elijah, by whom he was challenged and rebuked. Allowed his wife to take Naboth's vineyard in his name. Was victorious over Benhadad ; enticed Jehoshaphat into an alliance which ended in the latter's death. Was killed in fighting by "a bow at a venture" (I Kings xvi. 29). 2. A lying prophet (Jer. xxix. 21).

AHARAH—third son of Benjamin (I Chron. viii. 1).

AHARHEL—a son of Harum (I Chron. iv. 8).

AHASAI—a priest, son of Meshillemoth (Neh. xi. 13).

AHASBAI—one of David's heroes (II Sam. xxiii. 34).

AHASUERUS—a Persian king; husband of Esther (Esther i. 2).

AHAZ—a king of Judah who succeeded his father Jotham. Subsequently became a feudatory of Tiglath Pileser (II Kings xvi. 1).

AHAZIAH—1. Succeeded Ahaz as king of Israel; reigned for two years (I Kings xxii. 40). 2. Succeeded his father Joram as king of Judah. Called Jehoaz in II Chron. xxi. 17. (see also II Chron. xxii.1.)

AHI—1. A Gadite, son of Abdiel (I Chron. v. 15). 2. An Asherite, son of Shamer (I Chron. vii. 34).

AHIAH—1. Chief priest, grandson of Phinehas (I Sam. xv. 3). 2. A scribe of Solomon's reign (I Kings iv. 3).

AHIAM—one of David's mighty men (I Chron. xi. 35).

AHIAN—a Manassite (I Chron. vii. 19).

AHIEZER—1. A son of Ammishaddai (Num. i. 12). 2. A man of Gibeah (I Chron. xii. 3).

AHIHUD—a prince of the tribe of Asher (Num. xxxiv. 27).

AHIJAH—1. Son of Ehud (I Chron. ii. 25). 2. One of David's mighty men (I Chron. xi. 36). 3. A prophet of Shiloh (I Kings xi. 29). 4. A Levite (I Chron. xxvi. 20).

AHIKAM—son of Shaphan (II Kings xxv. 22).

AHILUD—father of Jehoshaphat (I Kings iv. 3).

AHIMAAZ—1. Father of Ahinoam (I Sam. xiv. 50). 2. Son of Zadok the high priest in David's time (II Sam. xv. 27).

AHIMAN—1. One of the sons of Anak (Num. xiii. 22). 2. A Levite (I Chron. ix. 17).

AHIMELECH—1. Chief priest at Nob in Saul's reign. Gave David the shewbread in answer to the latter's plea of hunger. Also gave him Goliath's sword (I Sam. xxi. 1). 2. Grandson of preceding (II Sam. viii. 7). 3. A Hittite follower of David (I Sam. xxvi. 6).

AHIMOTH—son of Elkanah (I Chron. vi. 25).

AHINADAB—purveyor to Solomon (I Kings iv. 14).

AHINOAM—1. Saul's wife (I Sam. xiv. 50). 2. A woman of Jezreel (I Sam. xxv. 43).

AHIO—1. Drove the cart in which the ark was carried (II Sam. vi. 3). 2. A Benjamite (I Chron. viii. 14).

AHIRA—son of Enan (Num. i. 15).

AHIRAM—a Benjamite (Num. xxvi. 38).

AHISAMACH—a Danite, father of Aholiab (Ex. xxxi. 6).

AHISHAHAR—son of Bilhan (I Chron. vii. 10).

AHISHAR—an officer in Solomon's household (I Kings iv. 6).

AHITOPHEL—one of David's counsellors. Clever but fickle. Sided with Absalom in the latter's rebellion. When his counsel was ignored he went home and committed suicide. Regarded as a type of Judas (II Sam. xv. 12).

AHITUB—grandson of Eli (I Sam. xiv. 3).

AHLAI—daughter of Sheshan (I Chron. ii. 31).

AHOAH—son of Bela (I Chron. viii. 4).

AHOLIAB—a Danite; a worker in the tabernacle (Ex. xxxi. 6).

AHUMAI—a man of Judah (I Chron. iv. 2).

AHUZAM—son of Ashur (I Chron. iv. 6).

AJAH—son of Zibeon (Gen. xxxvi. 24).

AKKUB—a Levite; porter at the king's gate (I Chron. ix. 17).

ALAMETH—a son of Becher (I Chron. vii. 8).

ALEMETH—son of Jehoadah (I Chron. viii. 36).

ALEXANDER—1. Son of Simon the Cyrenian (Mark xv. 21). 2. A Jerusalem ruler before whom Peter and John were brought for trial (Acts iv. 6). 3. A Jew with Paul at Ephesus (Acts xix. 33). 4. The " coppersmith " (II Tim. iv. 14).

ALMODAD—eldest son of Joktan (Gen. x. 26).

ALPHAEUS—1. Father of James the Less (Matt. x.3). 2. Father of Matthew (Mark ii. 14).

ALVAH—a duke of Edom (Gen. xxxvi. 40).

ALVAN—a Horite (Gen. xxxvi. 23).

AMAL—an Asherite (I Chron. vii. 35).

AMALEK—son of Eliphaz (Gen. xxxvi. 12).

AMALEKITES—descendants of above; long-standing enemies of Israel from earliest times till the death of their king, Agag, whom Samuel slew (I Sam. xv. 1 f.).

AMARIAH—1. A chief priest of Jehoshaphat's time (II. Chron. xix. 11). 2. Helped to distribute the free-will offerings of God in Hezekiah's time (II Chron. xxxi. 15).

AMASA—son of Ithra; captain of Absalom's army, after whose death he was forgiven and succeeded Joab as David's commander-in-chief (II Sam. xix. 13).

AMASAI—son of Elkanah (I Chron. vi. 25).

AMASHAI—a priest in Nehemiah's time (Neh. xi. 13).

AMASIAH—1. Son of Zichri. Held high office under Jehoshaphat (II Chron. xvii. 16). 2. King of Judah. Defeated the Edomites in the Valley of Salt. He then challenged Jehoash, King of Israel, to fight, but was heavily defeated in the battle of Bathshemesh. Reigned twentynine years and was finally murdered at Lachish (II Kings xiv. 1 f.).

AMITTAI—father of Jonah the prophet (Jonah i. 1).

AMMIEL—1. Son of Gemalli (Num. xiii. 12). 2. A man of Lodebar, father of Machir (II Sam. ix. 4). 3. Sixth son of Obed-edom (I Chron. xxvi. 5). 4. Another name for ELIAM.

AMMIHUD—1. Father of Elishama (I Chron. vi. 26). 2. Father of Shemuel (Num. xxxiv. 20). 3. Father of Talmai, king of Geshur (II Sam. xiii. 37).

AMMINADAB—1. Brother-in-law of Aaron (Ex. vi. 23). 2. Son of Uzziel (I Chron. xv. 10). 3. Son of Kohath (I Chron. vi. 22).

AMMISHADDAI—a Danite, father of Ahiezer (Num. i. 12).

AMMIZABAD—son of Benaiah (I Chron. xxvii. 6).

AMMON—Lot's younger son (Gen. xix. 38).

AMNON—a son of David. Murdered by Absalom on account of his treatment of Tamar (II Sam. xiii. 1).

AMON—1. Governor of Jerusalem (I Kings xxii. 26). 2. King of Judah, succeeding his father Manasseh at the age of 22. Was murdered in his palace two years later (II Kings xxi. 19 f.).

AMOS—a Judean prophet ; was a shepherd and grower of sycamore fruit. Bethel was the chief scene of his preaching. Amaziah, the chief priest there, sought to accuse him of treason, as possibly, the oppressed poor were roused by his stirring messages. On reaching his home he probably put his messages into words. We know little of his subsequent career, but he probably died a natural death at his own home (see his Book for references to his life).

AMOZ—the father of the prophet Isaiah (Isaiah i. 1).

AMPLIAS—a Christian of Rome (Rom. xvi. 8).

AMRAM—1. The father of Moses (Ex. vi. 20). 2. Son of Dishon (I Chron. i. 41).

AMRAPHEL—a king of Shinar who fought against Abraham (Gen. xiv. 1-9).

AMZI—1. A Levite (I Chron. vi. 46). 2. A priest, son of Zechariah (Neh. xi. 12).

ANAH—1. Mother-in-law of Esau (Gen. xxxvi. 2). 2. A " son " of Seir the Horite (Gen. xxxvi. 20).

ANAIAH—a supporter of Ezra (Neh. viii. 4).

ANAK—son of Arba, the progenitor of the Anakim or giants (Num. xiii. 22).

ANAN—one who covenanted with Nehemiah (Neh. x. 26).

ANANI—a son of Elioenai (I Chron. iii. 24).

ANANIAH—father of Maaseiah (Neh. iii. 23).

ANANIAS—1. One of the early Christians who " lied to the Holy Ghost " and was stricken dead as a punishment and a warning to others (Acts v. 1-11). 2. One sent to Paul at his conversion and who was a means of restoring Paul's sight (Acts ix. 10). 3. A high priest who judged Paul, and who was called by the Apostle " a whited wall." Went down to Cæsarea later as one of Paul's accusers (Acts xxiii. 2).

ANATH—father of Shamgar (Judg. iii. 31).

ANDREW—brother of Simon Peter and one of Christ's Apostles. He was first a disciple of John the Baptist. His life was characterised by quiet helpfulness. He found the " lad " at the feeding of the five thousand. He helped Philip to bring the Greeks to Jesus. Tradition says that his remains were brought to Scotland in a vessel that was wrecked off St. Andrew's Bay. He became the patron saint of Scotland, who adopted the St. Andrew's Cross (X) because St. Andrew was generally supposed to have been crucified on a cross so shaped (John i. 44).

ANDRONICUS—a Jewish Christian at Rome (Rom. xvi. 7).

ANER—an Amorite of Mamre (Gen. xiv. 13, 24).

ANIAM—a Manassite (I Chron. vii. 19).

ANNA—daughter of Phanuel; a prophetess who recognized the infant Jesus as the Messiah (Luke ii. 36).

ANNAS—high priest in the year that John the Baptist began his ministry. Father-in-law of Caiaphas. One of those who took part in the trial of Jesus (Luke iii. 2).

ANTIPAS—a martyr of Pergamos (Rev. ii. 12, 13).

ANTOTHIJAH—son of Shashak (a Benjamite) (I Chron. viii. 24).

ANUB—a man of Judah (I Chron. iv. 8).

APELLES—a Christian at Rome (Rom. xvi. 10).

APHIAH—an ancestor of King Saul (I Sam. ix. 1).

APOLLOS—a Jew, born at Alexandria. A disciple of John the Baptist, afterwards a teacher of Aquila and Priscilla at Ephesus. Very eloquent and was looked to by many as the leader of a " sect." This, however, does not seem to have been his intention. Some think he wrote the Epistle to the Hebrews (Acts xviii. 24-28).

APPAIM—younger son of Nadab (I Chron. ii. 30).

APPHIA—a woman who followed Paul's teaching (Philemon 2).

AQUILA—a Jew, born at Pontus ; husband of Priscilla. Prominent in the story of the early Church as a supporter of Paul (Acts xviii. 18).

ARAH—an Asherite (I Chron. vii. 39).

ARAM—1. Youngest son of Shem (Gen. x. 22). 2. An Asherite (I Chron. vii. 34). 3. A son of Machir (I Chron. ii. 23).

ARAN—a Horite duke (I Chron. i. 42).

ARAUNAH—a Jebusite, in whose custody the Ark rested for a time (II Sam. xxiv. 18-25).

ARBAH—father of Anak (Gen. xxxv. 27).

ARCHELAUS—elder son of Herod the Great ; brought up at Rome. He was considered the worst of all Herod's line, and the

Samaritans could not en-
dure his administration.
A parable of Christ's seems
to refer to him (Matt.
ii. 22).

ARCHIPPUS—a Christian
at Colosse, called by St.
Paul his " fellow-soldier "
(Col. iv. 17).

ARD—grandson of Benjamin
(Gen. xlvi. 21).

ARDON—son of Calab (I
Chron. ii. 18).

ARELI—son of Gad (Num.
xxvii. 17).

ARETAS—s u c c e s s f u l l y
waged war against Herod
the Tetrarch as an out-
come of Herod's treatment
of A.'s daughter. He held
Damascus for a time (II
Cor. xi. 32).

ARIDAI—a son of Haman
(Esther ix. 9).

ARIEL—a Jew with Ezra at
the Brook Ahava (Ezra
viii. 16).

ARIOCH—1. King of Ella-
sar (Gen. xiv. 1-9). 2.
Captain of the king's guard
under Nebuchadnezzar
(Dan. ii. 14).

ARISAI—a son of Haman
(Esther ix. 9).

ARISTARCHUS—a Mace-
donian from Thessalonica,
with Paul (Acts xix. 29).

ARISTOBULUS—a Christ-
ian who sent salutations
to Paul (Rom. xvi. 10).

ARMONI—one of Saul's sons
(II Sam. xxi. 8).

ARODI—a son of Gad (Gen.
xlvi. 16).

ARPHAXAD—third son of
Shem, and the representa-
tive of Chaldea (Gen. x.
22).

ARTAXERXES—(c a l l e d
" The Long-handed ")
reigned 464-465 B.C. over
Persia. Sent Ezra, and
afterwards Nehemiah, back
to aid in the reconstruction
of Jerusalem (see the Books
of Ezra and Nehemiah).

ARTEMAS—a companion of
Paul (Titus iii. 12).

ARTEMIS—the Greek god-
dess of hunting (Acts xix.
24, RV.). Another name
for Diana (which see).

ARZA—the steward of King
Elah's house in Tirzah
(I Kings xvi. 9).

ASA—King of Juda, son of
Abijah, and grandson of
Rehoboam. A religious
reformation, accompanied
by the destruction of
images, took place during
his reign (I Kings xv. 9,
etc.).

ASAHEL—1. Son of Jeruiah
and brother of Joab and
Abishai. One of David's
military captains (I Chron.
xxvii. 7). 2. A Levite
under Jehoshaphat (II
Chron. xvii. 8).

ASAIAH.—1. A Simeonite
prince (I Chron. iv. 36).
2. A man of Judah (I
Chron. ix. 5).

ASAPH—A Levite " of high
musical gifts." The name
of one of the three guilds
which conducted the
musical services of the
temple. (Neh. vii. 44.)
They were at first the
backbone of the temple
choir, and later they shared
these services with the
" sons of Korah." Psalms
l. and lxxxiii. have the
superscription "to
Asaph."

ASAREEL—a man of Judah
(I Chron. iv. 16).

ASARELAH—a son of Asaph (I Chron. xxv. 2).

ASENATH—the daughter of Potipherah, priest of On, who became the wife of Joseph and the mother of Manasseh and Ephraim (Gen. xli. 50).

ASHBEA—a descendant of Shelah, of the tribe of Judah (I Chron. iv. 21).

ASHBEL—third son of Benjamin (Gen. xlvi. 21).

ASHER—eighth son of Jacob (Gen xlvi. 17).

ASHKENAZ—the eldest son of Gomer (Gen. x. 3).

ASHPENAZ—the master of the eunuchs during Nebuchadnezzar's reign (Dan. i. 3).

ASHTORETH—the principal goddess of the Sidonians (I Kings xi. 5).

ASHUR—a son of Hezron and termed "father of Tekoa" (I Chron. ii. 24).

ASIEL—a Simeonite (I Chron. iv. 35).

ASNAH—a Jew, some of whose descendants returned from the Babylonian exile (Ezra ii. 50).

ASNAPPER—a high Assyrian dignitary (Ezra iv. 10).

ASPATHA—a son of Haman (Esther ix. 7).

ASRIEL—a son of Manasseh (Num. xxvi. 31).

ASSHUR—second son of Shem (Gen. x. 22).

ASSIR—a second son of Korah (I Chron. vi. 23).

ASYNCRITUS—a Christian at Rome (Rom. xvi. 14).

ATARAH—one of the wives of Jerahmeel (I Chron. ii. 26).

ATER—ninety-eight of his descendants returned from the Babylonian exile (Ezra ii. 16).

ATHAIAH—a man of Judah (Neh. xi. 4).

ATHALIAH—1. The daughter of Ahab, and granddaughter of Omri (II Kings xi. 1-16). Followed in the footsteps of her mother Jezebel. Was unscrupulous and cruel, shedding blood unhesitatingly to accomplish her desires. Was ultimately killed at the entrance to her palace. 2. A Benjamite (I Chron. viii. 26).

ATHLAI—a son of Bebai (Ezra x. 28).

AUGUSTUS—the first Roman Emperor; called in the New Testament, Cæsar Augustus (Luke ii. 1).

AZALIAH—the father of Shaphan (II Chron. xxxiv. 8).

AZANIAH—a Levite; father of Jeshua (Neh. x. 9).

AZAREEL—1. A singer in David's time (I Chron. xxv. 18). 2. A priest, son of Ahasai (Neh. xi. 13).

AZARIAH—a very common name in the Old Testament, applied as follows: a son of Ethan (I Chron. ii. 8); a priest, son of Ahimaaz (I Chron. vi. 9); a son of Nathan (I Kings iv. 5); a priest, son of Johanan (I Chron. vi. 10); a prophet, son of Oded (II Chron. xv. 1-8); a son of Jehoshaphat (II Chron. xxi. 2); a man of Judah (I Chron. ii. 38); an Ephraimite (II Chron. xxviii. 12); a king of Judah, better known as

Uzziah (which *see*) (II Kings xv. 1) ; the leader of a body of priests (II Chron. xxvi 17) ; the chief priest of the house of Zadok (II Chron. xxxi. 10) ; a Kohathite Levite (I Chron. vi. 36) ; a Merarite Levite (II Chron. xxix. 12) ; a priest, son of Hilkiah (I Chron. vi. 13) ; a son of Hoshaiah (Jer. xliii. 2) ; the original name of Abednego (Dan. i. 7) ; a prince of Judah (Neh. xii. 33) ; a son of Maaseiah (Neh. iii. 23) ; a teacher appointed by Ezra (Neh. viii. 7) ; and one or two others.

AZAZ—a Reubenite, son of Shema (I Chron. v. 8).

AZAZIAH—1. A harper during David's reign (I Chron. xv. 21). 2. An overseer of the Temple (II Chron. xxxi. 13).

AZEL—a descendant of Jonathan (I Chron. viii. 37).

AZGAD—head of a family in Nehemiah's time (Ezra ii. 12).

AZMAVATH—one of David's mighty men (II Sam. xxiii. 31).

AZMAVETH—a son of Jehoadah (I Chron. viii. 36).

AZRIEL—1. A Naphtalite (I Chron. xxvii. 19). 2. The father of Seraiah (Jer. xxxvi, 26).

AZRIKAM—1. The eldest son of Azel (I Chron. viii. 38). 2. The governor of the palace under King Ahaz (II Chron. xxviii. 7).

AZUBAH—the wife of Caleb (I Chron. ii. 18).

AZUR—1. A Gibeonite, father of the prophet Hananiah (Jer. xxviii. 1). 2. The father of Jaazaniah, " who devised wickedness " (Ezek. xi. 1).

AZZAN—father of Paltiel (Num. xxxiv. 26).

AZZUR—one who signed the " covenant " with Nehemiah (Neh. x. 17).

B

BAAL—the Semetic deity of " fertility," whose cult was unsparingly denounced by the Hebrew prophets because of its gross sensuality (Num. xxii. 41 & Judg. vi. 25). *Variants*, Bel, Beel.

BAAL-BERITH—the Canaanite deity of Shechem, idolatrously worshipped by the Israelites on the death of Gideon (Judg. viii. 33).

BAAL-HANAN—1. A king of Edom (Gen. xxxvi. 38). 2. A Gederite (I Chron. xxvii. 28).

BAALI—an appellation forbidden to be applied to Jehovah (Hos. ii. 16).

BAALIM—plural of Baal ; idols, masters, or false gods (Judg. ii. 11).

BAALIS—a king of the Ammonites (Jer. xl. 14).

BAAL-PEOR—the Moabite god at Peor (probably Chemosh) to whose corrupt worship the Israelites were drawn away from Jehovah (Num. xxv. 3).

BAANA—1. Name of two officials of Solomon (I Kings iv. 12). 2. Father of Zadok (Neh. iii. 4).

BAANAH—I. Father of Heleb, the latter was a warrior of David's (II Sam. xxiii. 29). 2. An officer of Ish-bosheth, the son of Saul (II Sam. iv. 12).

BAARA—a wife of Shaharaim (I Chron. viii. 8).

BAASEIAH—Levite ancestor of Asaph (I Chron. vi. 40).

BAASHA—the third king of Israel (I Kings xv. 16 ff.).

BAKBAKKAR—head of a Levite family (I Chron. ix. 15).

BAKBUK—founder of a family of Nethinim who returned from exile with Zerubbabel (Ezra ii. 51.).

BAKBUKIAH—a Levite (a porter), of the sons of Asaph (Neh. xi. 17).

BALAAM—the son of Beor and a magician (soothsayer) of Pethor, called by Balak, king of Moab, to curse the Israelites (Num. xxii. 5 ff.). The narrative in *Numbers* presents some incongruities in the character of the old heathen enchanter, probably explained by the mixed documentary sources which supply the story.

BALAK—king of Moab, famous for having hired Balaam (Num. xxii. 2).

BANI—1. A Gidite, one of David's heroes (II Sam. xxiii. 36). 2. A Merarite (I Chron. vi. 46). 3. A Judahite (I Chron. ix. 4). 4. 5. Levites (Neh. iii. 17 ff.). 6. A post-exilic family (Ezra ii. 10).

BARABBAS—a noted criminal, released by Pilate as an act of clemency when Jesus was arraigned (Mark xv. 7).

BARACHEL—father of Elihu (Job xxxii. 2).

BARAK—son of Abinoam ; shares with Deborah the glory of defeating Sisera (Judg. iv. 6).

BARIAH—son of Shemaiah (I Chron. iii. 22).

BAR-JESUS—A certain Jewish magician and false prophet, stricken with temporary blindness for interfering with Paul's work on his visit to Cyprus (Acts xiii. 6 ff.) *Variant*, Elymas (Magus).

BAR-JONA—*see* Peter (Matt. xvi. 17).

BARKOS—ancestor of a family of Nethinim who returned from exile with Zerubbabel (Ezra ii, 53).

BARNABAS—the surname given by the Apostles to Joseph, the Cyprian-Levite —a great friend and helper of Paul in his missionary work (Acts iv. 36).

BARSABAS—1. *Joseph ;* introduced with Matthias (which *see*) for Apostleship as successor to Judas (Acts i. 23). 2. *Judas ;* an official of the church at Jerusalem (Acts xv. 22).

BARTHOLOMEW—one of the twelve Apostles, with whom Nathanael is sometimes mistakenly identified (Mark iii. 18).

BARTIMÆUS—blind son of Timæus ; healed by Jesus (Mark. x. 46).

BARUCH—1. Son of Neriah ; he read Jeremiah's "roll" to the people (Jer. xxxii ; 12 ; xxxvi. 4). 2. One of those who repaired the wall of Jerusalem (Neh. iii. 20). 3. One of those who signed the covenant (Neh. x. 6). 4. The son of Col-hozeh (Neh. xi. 5).

BARZILLAI—1. A wealthy chieftain who befriended David when he fled from Absalom (II Sam. xvii. 27). 2. Father of Adriel (II Sam. ii. 21). 3. Ancestor of a family of priests (Ezra ii. 61).

BASEMATH—1. One of the wives of Esau (Gen. xxvi. 34). 2. A daughter of Solomon (I Kings iv. 15).

BATH-SHEBA—wife of Uriah ; committed adultery with David, to whom afterwards she was married (II Sam. xi. 2 ff.).

BAVAI—son of Henadad, helped to repair wall of Jerusalem (Neh. iii. 18). (see Binnui.)

BAZLUTH—ancestor of a family of Nethinim (Ezra ii. 52). *Variant*, Bazlith.

BEALIAH—a Benjamite, one of David's soldiers (I Chron. xii. 5).

BEBAI—founder of a large post-exilic family (Ezra ii. 11).

BECHER—1. Son of Benjamin (Gen. xlvi. 21). 2. Son of Ephraim, ancestral head of the Becherites (Num. xxvi. 35). *Variant*, Bered (I Chron. vii. 20).

BECORATH—ancestor of Saul (I Sam. ix. 1).

BEDAD—father of Hadad, king of Edom (Gen. xxvi. 35).

BEDAN—1. Mentioned as one of the early deliverers of Israel—possibly confused with Barak (I Sam.

xii. 11). 2. Head of a Manassite family (I Chron. vii. 17).

BEDEIAH—one of the sons of Bani (Ezra x. 35).

BEELIADA—a son of David (I Chron. xiv. 7). *Variant*, Eliada.

BEELZEBUB—Hebrew form of Baalzebub—a Philistine deity, " the god of flies " (II Kings i. 2 ff.).

BEERA—a son of Zophar (I Chron. vii. 3).

BEERAH—a Reubenite prince, taken captive by Tiglath-pilneser (I Chron. v. 6). *Variant*, pileser.

BEERI—1. Hittite, father of Judith, one of Esau's wives (Gen. xxvi. 34). 2. Father of Hosea, prophet (Hos. i. 1).

BEL—*originally*, Baal—a great Babylonian deity (Jer. l. 2).

BELA—1. A king of Edom (Gen. xxxvi. 32 ff.). 2. Ancestral head of one of the clans (Belaites) of Benjamin (Gen. xlvi. 21). 3. A Reubenite, ancestral head of one of the clans (I Chron. v. 8 ff.).

BELIAL—*primarily* in a neutral sense to mean "unprofitable," or "worthless " (Deut. xiii. 13) ; but *later* personified and identified as the genius of all evil (II Cor. vi. 15).

BELSHAZZAR—successor of Nebuchadnezzar, and last Chaldean king of Babylon (Dan. v. 1).

BELTESHAZZAR—the Babylonian name conferred on Daniel (Dan. i. 7).

BEN—a Levite (I Chron. xv. 18).

BEN-ABINADAB—son of Abinadab and an officer under Solomon (I Kings iv. 11, *margin*).

BENAIAH—1. Son of . Jehoiada; one of David's brave captains (II Sam. xxiii. 20 ff.). 2. A Pirathonite, another of David's thirty heroes (II Sam. xxiii. 30). 3. A Simeonite (I Chron. iv. 36). 4. A Levite (I Chron. xv. 18 ff.). 5. A priest (I Chron. xv. 24). 6. A forefather of Jahaziel (II Chron. xx. 14). 7. Several obscure persons (*see* II Chron. xxxi. 13, Ezek. xi. 1 ff., Ezra x. 25 ff.).

BEN-DEKER—an officer under Solomon (I Kings iv. 9, *margin*).

BEN-GEBER—" son of Geber," one of Solomon's officers (I Kings iv. 13, *margin*).

BEN-HADAD—names of three kings of Damascus : 1. Son of Tabrimmon (I Kings xv. 18). 2. Son of preceding (I Kings xx. 1 ff.). 3. Son of Haziel (II Kings xiii. 3 ff.).

BEN-HAIL—a prince of Judah, appointed " teacher " by Jehoshaphat (II Chron. xvii. 7).

BEN-HANAN—son of Shimon (I Chron. iv. 20).

BEN-HESED—an officer under Solomon (I Kings iv. 10, *margin*).

BEN-HUR—an officer under Solomon (I Kings iv. 8, *margin*).

BENINU—a Levite, one of those who sealed the covenant (Neh. x. 13).

BENJAMIN—1. Youngest son of Jacob—named by Rachel, Ben-oni (Gen. xxxv. 18). 2. Son of Bilhan and great-grandson of Benjamin (I Chron. vii. 10). 3. One of the " sons of Harim " (Ezra x. 32).

BENO—son of Merari (I Chron. xxiv. 26 ff.).

BEN-ONI—*see* Benjamin.

BEN-ZOHETH—son of Ishi (I Chron. iv. 20).

BEOR—1. Father of Balaam (Num. xxii. 5). 2. Father of Bela, king of Edom (Gen. xxxvi. 32).

BERA—king of Sodom (Gen. xiv. 2).

BERACHAH—a Benjamite who joined David at Ziklag (I Chron. xii. 3). *Variant*, Beracah.

BERACHIAH—1. Father of Asaph (I Chron. vi. 39). *Variant*, Berechiah. 2. A Levite guard of the Ark (I Chron. xv. 23). 3. Son of Zerubbabel (I Chron. iii. 20). 4. Father of Zechariah (Zech. i. 1). 5. Father of Meshullam (Neh. iii. 4). 6. Ephraimite chief (II Chron. xxviii. 12).

BERAIAH—a Benjamite, one of the sons of Shimei (I Chron. viii. 21).

BERI—head of a family of Asher (I Chron. vii. 36).

BERIAH—1. Son of Asher (Gen. xlvi. 17). 2. A Benjamite (I Chron. viii 13). 3. Son of Shimei (I Chron. xxiii. 10). ' 4. Son of Ephraim (I Chron. vii. 23).

BERNICE—daughter of Herod Agrippa I, thrice married (Acts xxv. 13 ff.). *Variant*, Berenice.

BERODACH-BALADAN—

a king of Babylon (II Kings xx. 12) (*see* Merodach-Baladan).

BESAI—ancestral head of a Nethinim family (Ezra ii. 49).

BESODEIAH—father of Meshullam (Neh. iii. 6).

BETHUEL—son of Nahor, father of Rebekah, Isaac's wife (Gen. xxii. 22 ff.).

REZAI—ancestral head of a post-exilic family (Ezra ii. 17).

BEZALEEL—1. Son of Uri, son of Hur, chief artificer of tabernacle (Ex. xxxi. 2 ff.). 2. One of the sons of Pahath-moab (Ezra x. 30).

BEZER—head of a family of Asher (I Chron. vii. 37).

BICHRI—" Sheba the Bichrite," who revolted from David, is called the " son " of Bichri (II Sam. xx. 1 ff.).

BIDKAR—officer of Jehu (II Kings ix. 25).

BIGTHA—eunuch of Ahasuerus (Esther i. 10).

BIGTHAN—Bigthana — eunuch who plotted against Ahasurus (Esther. ii. 21).

BIGVAI—1. Companion of Zerubbabel (Ezra ii. 2). 2. Representatives of this family who sealed the covenant (Neh. x. 16).

BILDAD—one of Job's friends (Job ii. 11).

BILGAH—1. Ancestral head of the fifteenth course of priests (I Chron. xxiv. 14). 2. A priest; returned from exile with Zerubbabel (Neh. xii. 5). *Variant,* Bilgai.

BILGAI—*See* Bilgah.

BILHAH—a slave girl of Rachael's (Gen. xxiix. 29).

BILHAN—1. A Horite chief. son of Ezer (Gen. xxxv,)

27). 2. A descendant of Benjamin (I Chron. vii. 10).

BILSHAN—a leader under Zerubbabel (Ezra ii. 2).

BIMHAL—son of Japhlet, and a descendant of Asher (I Chron. vii. 33).

BINEA—son of Moza and a descendant of Jonathan (I Chron. viii. 37).

BINNUI—1. Ancestral head of one of the post-exilic families (Neh. vii. 15). 2. A Levite (Ezra viii. 33). 3. Son of Pahath-moab (Ezra x. 30). 4. Son of Bani (Ezra x. 38). *Variants,* Bani, Bunni, Bavai.

BIRSHA—king of Gomorrah (Gen. xiv. 2).

BISHLAM—a Persian officer (Ezra iv. 7).

BITHIAH—daughter of a Pharaoh and wife of Mered (I Chron. iv. 18).

BIZTHA—eunuch of Ahasuerus (Esther i. 10).

BLASTUS—chamberlain of Herod Agrippa I (Acts xii. 20).

BOANERGES — appellation given by Jesus to James and John, interpreted as " sons of thunder " (Mark iii. 17).

BOAZ—wealthy citizen of Bethlehem, son of Salmon ; important, as from his levirate marriage with Ruth sprang Jesse, the father of David (Ruth vi. 21 ff.).

BOCHERU—a descendant of Jonathan (I Chron. viii. 38).

BOHAN—son of Reuben (Josh. xv. 6).

BUKKI—1. Son of Jogli, a Danite (Num. xxxiv. 22). 2. A priest, son of Abishua (I Chron. vi. 5).

BUKKIAH—a Levite musician, son of Heman (I Chron. xxv. 4).

BUNAH—son of Jerahmeel (I Chron. ii. 25).

BUNNI—*see* Binnui.

BUZ—1. Son of Nahor and Milcah, and nephew of Abraham (Gen. xxii. 21). 2. A descendant of tribe of Gad (I Chron. v. 14).

BUZI—father of prophet Ezekiel (Ezek. i. 3).

C

CÆSAR—the name adopted by Octavius, afterwards called Augustus. Cæsar became the official title of the Roman emperors until the third century A.D. The following Cæsars fall within New Testament times : Augustus, 31 B.C.-A.D. 14 ; Tiberius, A.D. 14-37 ; Gaius (Caligula), A.D. 37-41 ; Claudius, A.D. 41-54 ; Nero, A.D. 54-68 ; Galba, A.D. 68-69 ; Otho, A.D. 69 ; Vitellius, A.D. 69 ; Vespasian, A.D. 69-79 ; Titus, A.D. 79-81 ; Domitian, A.D. 81-96. Four of these are mentioned in the New Testament : Augustus (Luke ii. 1) ; Tiberius (Luke iii. 1) ; Claudius (Acts xi. 28 and xviii. 2) ; Nero (Phil. v. 22, II Tim. iv. 16, 17).

CAIAPHAS—High priest in the days of Jesus. Son-in-law to Annas. Counselled the putting of Jesus to death before a tumult of the people should arise. He had a characteristic disregard of justice, and was in a large degree respon-sible for the death of Jesus (John xi. 49-53).

CAIN—the eldest son of Adam and Eve, who, according to the ancient story of *Genesis*, was made a "fugitive" and "wanderer" as a punishment for having slain his brother, Abel, being moved to this wicked deed by implacable jealousy—envious of his brother's good (Gen. iv.ff.).

[It should be noted that there is a later Cain, quite distinct from the "fugitive" —referred to in *Genesis* iv. 16 ff.—who built a city and became a promogenitor in one of the great genealogical lines of descent.]

Some consider that the "sign" put upon Ca' was in all probability t' "totem sign" of the · _ of Cain, and, indeed, that the whole story enshrines some primitive tribal struggle for the mastery in the very earliest ages of the world's history—though it must not be forgotten that the New Testament would appear to give credence to the story as relating to Cain, by recording that Cain slew his brother because he of his goodness offered to the Creator a more excellent sacrifice than his own (I John iii. 12, and Hebrews xi. 4).

CALEB—1. Son of Hezron, third in direct descent from Judah. (I Chron. ii. 18.) 2. Son of Jephunneh. First appears as the spy chosen to represent Judah. He

and Joshua brought back a faithful report which was not accepted. Was allowed to survive the rest of his people that he and Joshua might enter into the Promised Land. He received Hebron as his portion after he had expelled the giants therefrom (Num. xiii. 6).

CANAAN—fourth son of Ham ; progenitor of the Canaanites ; was "cursed" as a consequence of his father's sin. He was to be " a servant of servants " to his brethren (Gen. ix. 25).

CANDACE—a queen of Ethiopia. A eunuch of her court was converted to Christianity by Philip the Evangelist (Acts viii. 27).

CARMI—1. Youngest son of Reuben (Gen. xlvi. 9). 2. Son of Zabdi and father of Achan (Josh. vii. 1).

CARPUS—a resident of Troas with whom Paul left his cloak (II Tim. iv. 13).

CARSHENA—one of the seven leading princes of Persia at the court of Ahasuerus (Esther i. 14).

CASTOR & POLLUX—two Greek and Roman divinities having the same mother (Leda). Also the name of the Alexandrian vessel in which Paul sailed from " Melita " to Rome (Acts xxviii. 11).

CEPHAS—another name for Simon Peter (Aramaic for " a rock ") (John i. 42).

CHEDORLAOMER—a king of Elam who fought against Abraham in the Jordan valley (Genesis xiv. 1-16).

CHELAL—a son of Pahathmoab (Ezra x. 30).

CHELLUH—a son of Bani (Ezra x. 35).

CHELUB—a man of Judah (I Chron. iv. 11).

CHEMOSH—an idol worshipped by the Moabites and Ammonites (Num. xxi. 29).

CHENAANAH—1. A Benjamite, son of Bilhan (I Chron. vii. 10). 2. The father of Zedekiah (I Kings xxii. 11).

CHENANI—a Levite who helped to lead the exiles into a covenant with Jehovah (Neh. ix. 4).

CHENANIAH—a singer, chief of the Levites in David's time (I Chron. xv. 22).

CHERAN—a Horite, son of Dishon (Gen. xxxvi. 26).

CHERUB—(plural cherubim or cherubs, but cherubiim is a double plural). One of the angelic beings set to guard the gate of Paradise (Gen. iii. 24).

CHESED—a son of Nahor (Gen. xxii. 22).

CHILEAB—David's second son, born at Hebron; also called Daniel (II Sam. iii. 3).

CHILION—the younger son of Elimelech and Naomi (Ruth i. 2).

CHIMHAM—son of Barzillai the Gileadite (II Sam. xix. 37).

CHISLON—father of Elidad (Num. xxxiv. 21).

CHLOE—a Christian woman, apparently the head of a house at Corinth (I Cor. i. 11).

CHRIST—the Anointed One.

Greek *equivalent* of Hebrew " Messiah." Borrowed from the Septuagint (Psalm ii. 2 ; Dan. ix. 25. etc.). When so used in the New Testament it generally has " the " prefixed. Became almost part of the name for Jesus to whom the combined title of Jesus Christ is often applied (Matt. xvi. 16) (*see* also JESUS CHRIST.

CHUZA—Herod the Tetrarch's steward whose wife Joanna ministered to the wants of Jesus (Luke viii. 3).

CLAUDIA—a female Christian who joined with Paul in sending a salutation to Timothy (II Tim. iv. 21).

CLAUDIUS—the fourth Roman Emperor (*see* " Cæsar ").

CLAUDIUS LYSIAS—the chief captain at Jerusalem when Paul was brought to trial there (Acts xi. 28 and xxiii. 26).

CLEMENT—a Christian who laboured with Paul (Phil. iv. 3).

CLEOPAS—one of the two disciples who met with Christ on the road to Emmaus (Luke xxiv. 18).

CLEOPHAS (or Clopas)—same as Alphæus (John xix. 25).

COL-HOZEH—father of Shallum and Baruch (Neh. iii. 15).

CONONIAH—a Levite who had charge of the tithes, etc., under Hezekiah (II Chron. xxxi. 12).

CORNELIUS—one of the centurions of the Italian band stationed at Cæsarea.

A devout man who sent to Joppa for Peter, who came and taught him. Was in a manner the " first-fruits " of the Gentiles (Acts x. 1-48).

COZ—a man of Judah (I Chron. iv. 8).

COZBI—a Midianitish woman, slain by Phinehas (Num. xxv. 15).

CRESCENS—a Christian with Paul for a time at Rome (II Tim. iv. 10).

CRISPUS—the ruler of the Jewish synagogue at Corinth (Acts xviii. 8).

CUSH—1. Eldest son of Ham (Gen. x. 6). 2. A Benjamite foe of King David (Psalm vii. *title*).

CUSHAN (Cushan-Rishathaim)—a king of Mesopotamia into whose hands the Israelites were delivered as a punishment for their idolatry (Judg. iii. 8).

CUSHI—father of Zephaniah (Zeph. i. 1).

CYRUS—a king whom Isaiah predicted was to gain great victories, and who was to free the Israelites from their Babylonian captivity. Cyrus in the first year of his reign issued a proclamation permitting Jews to return to their own land, and urging them to rebuild the Temple (*see* Isaiah xliv. 28 ; xlv., also Ezra i. 1-11).

D

DAGON—a Philistine deity whose origin and identity are uncertain, but whose cult was fairly ancient

and wide-spread. He de-
volved from a fish-god or
agricultural deity into a
war-god (Judg. xvi. 21 ff.).
DALAIAH—1. A son of Eli-
oenai (1 Chron. iii. 24).
2. A priest, head of 23rd
course (I Chron. xxiv. 18).
3. Son of Shemaiah (Jer.
xxxvi. 12). 4. Head of a
post-exilic family (Ezra
ii. 60). 5. Son of Mehetabeel (Neh. vi. 10). *Variant*,
Delaiah.

DALPHON—son of Haman
(Esther ix. 7).

DAMARIS—a woman of up-
per class, converted under
Paul at Athens (Acts xvii.
34).

DAN—son of Jacob by Bil-
hah, Rachel's maid (Gen.
xxx. 6).

DANIEL—1. Son of David
and Abigail (I Chron. iii. 1).
2. A priest, son of Ithamar,
one who returned with
Ezra from exile (Ezra
viii. 2). 3. A pious sage
equated by Ezekiel with
Noah and Job (Ezek. xiv.
14). Doubtless identical
with the great prophet
Daniel (Ezek. xxviii. 3,
and Book of *Daniel*).

DARDA—a man of prover-
bial wisdom (I Kings iv. 31).
Variant, Dara.

DARIUS—1. Darius Hystas-
pes, who allowed the Jews
to rebuild the temple (Ez.
vi. 6 ff.). 2. " Darius the
Persian "—identity uncer-
tain, probably the great
Darius (Neh. xii. 22). 3.
" Darius the Mede "—iden-
tity uncertain : said to
be the son of Ahasuerus ;
successor of Belshazzer

as king of Babylon. (Dan.
v. 31).

DARKON—ancestral head
of one of the post-exilic
families (Ezra ii. 56).

DATHAN—a Reubenite,
whose name is linked up
with Korah and Abiram in
the rebellion against Moses
(Num. xvi 1 ff.). (*see* Korah).

DAVID—the shepherd son of
Jesse, a farmer of Bethlehem, who became king of
Judah and Israel, and who
typifies the Messiah and
spiritual head of his Church
(I Sam. xvii. 13 ff.). His
name signifies " beloved,"
and the details of his life
may be summarized under
four headings : Shepherd,
Singer, Soldier, Sovereign ;
and it is supposed that the
biblical narratives covering
his wonderful career have
been gathered from various
sources and fused together
in the records given in
I and II Sam. (text re-
garded as somewhat cor-
rupt) and I Kings. His
personal character shows
him to be a man of the
age in which he lived—a
strange complex of good
and evil : while his public
career moves on a highly
dramatic plane—as ruler,
law-giver, warrior, musi-
cian (though none of the
Psalms can be definitely
assigned to his authorship),
father, king, he shines out
as one of the greatest of the
national heroes of God's
chosen people.

DEBIR—king of Eglon, put
to death by Joshua for rebellion (Josh. x. 3).

DEBORAH—1. Name of Rebekah's nurse (Gen. xxxv. 8). 2. A " prophetess," one of the " judges " of Israel, identified herself with Barak in delivering Israel from the Canaanites under Jabin and Sisera (Judg. iv. 4 ff.).

DEDAN—a people of North Arabia, descendants from Cush (Gen. x. 7).

DEHAVITES—identification uncertain, but probably settlers in Samaria by King Asnapper (Ezra iv. 9).

DELAIAH—see Dalaiah.

DELILAH—Samson's Philistine mistress, who betrayed him (Judg. vi. 4 ff.).

DEMAS—a companion and co-worker of Paul, but later a turn-coat (Col. iv. 14).

DEMETRIUS—1. A silversmith in Ephesus, ringleader in a riot against Paul (Acts xix. 24). 2. A disciple, who was commended by the apostle John (III John 12).

DEUEL—a Gadite, father of Eliasaph, a prince of Israel (Num. i. 14).

DEVIL—" the adversary " of God and of men ; in a general sense, a malignant being of superhuman personality and power, who places himself in another's way in order to oppose him ; in a definite sense, the spirit of evil, the accuser at law, the traducer of men (Gen. iii. ; Zech. iii. 1-2). The primitive and Jewish conception, associated more or less with the idea of " demons," gave way to foreign influences, especially to Babylonian and Greek, and developing slowly there emerged the full biblical conception (later Judaistic and New Testament) of a supreme personal spirit possessed of surpassing wisdom and malice, the enemy of God and the tempter of men : his functions are seen active in tempting Jesus, in nullifying good, as the instigator of falsehood, the enticer of men into sin and the instrument of corrective punishment where men violate righteousness—as the bringer of bondage and death into the world, he is the very antithesis to Christ. The doctrine of Satan has its parallels in most mythologies of the Pagan nations —as Norse (Loki), Persian (Ahriman), Greek (Momus), Babylonian (Tiâmat), etc. Scriptural variants, Satan, Beelzebub, Belial, " prince of the demons," "prince of this world and of the power of the air," and " the old serpent." (see Satan).

DIANA—a goddess of Ephesus, whose cult was centred around a rude, meteoric stone idol said to have fallen from heaven (Acts xix. 23 ff.). Identified somewhat erroneously with both the Greek and the Asiatic forms of the divinity, Artemis (which see).

DIBLAIM—father of Hosea's wife, Gomer (Hos. i. 3).

DIBRI—a Danite, father of Shelomith (Lev. xxiv. 11).

DIDYMUS—*see* Thomas.

DINAH—daughter of Jacob by Leah (according to Gen. xxx. 21—authenticity doubtful).

DIONYSIUS—one of Paul's converts in Athens (Acts xvii. 34).

DIOTREPHES—a peevishly ambitious person brought into prominence entirely by his obstinate refusal to recognize properly constituted authority in the Church (III John 9).

DISHON—a name or names representing an individual or a clan (Gen. xxxvi. 21 ff.). *Variant,* Dishan.

DODO—1. The forefather of Tola, one of the judges (Judg. x. 1). 2. A Bethlehemite, one of David's "mighty men," father of Elhanan (II Sam. xxiii. 24). 3. One of David's heroes, and father of Eleazer. (II Sam. xxiii. 9. cf., I Chron. xi. 26 and II Sam. xxi. 19).

DOEG—an Edomite, one of Saul's chief servants (I Sam. xxi. 7).

DORCAS—The Greek name of a Christian woman in Joppa, held in repute for her "good works" (Acts ix. 36 ff.).

E

EBAL—a son of Shobal (Gen. xxxvi. 23).

EBED—1. The father of Gaal (Judg. ix. 28). 2. A Jew who returned with Ezra (Ezra viii. 6).

EBED-MELECH—an Ethiopian who drew Jeremiah out of the pit (Jer. xxxviii. 7).

EBER—1. Father of Peleg and Joktan (Gen. x. 21). 2. A priest who returned from Babylon with Zerubbabel (Neh. xii. 20).

EDER—a son of Mushi, of the family of Merari (I Chron. xxiii. 23).

EDOM—another name for Esau. Given when he asked for "red" (Edom) pottage (Gen. xxv. 30).

EGLAH—one of David's wives (II Sam. iii. 5).

EGLON—King of Moab, assassinated by Ehud (Judg. iii. 12).

EHUD—1. A son of Bilhan (I Chron. vii. 10). 2. A left-handed Benjamite who assassinated Eglon (above). He then led a national rebellion, slaying 10,000 Moabites at the ford of Jordan. He became a "judge" of Israel (Judg. iii. 15).

ELADAH—a descendant of Ephraim (I Chron. vii. 20).

ELAH—1. Father of Shimei (I Kings iv. 18). 2. A son of Caleb (I Chron. iv. 15). 3. Son and successor of Baasha in the kingdom of Israel. He reigned about two years, and was assassinated whilst "drinking himself drunk in the house of Arza" (I Kings xvi. 6). 4. The father of Hoshea, king of Israel (II Kings xv. 30).

ELAM—1. Eldest son of Shem (Gen. x. 22). 2. Head of a family or clan, many of whom returned from Babylon with Zerubbabel (Ezra ii. 7). 3. One

of the priests who took part in the dedication of the wall of Jerusalem (Neh. xii. 42).

ELASAH—1. A son of Shaphan : carried a letter from Jeremiah at Jerusalem, to the exiles at Babylon (Jer. xxix. 3). 2. A son of Pashur (Ezra x. 22).

ELDAAH—youngest son of Midian, and grandson of Abraham (Gen. xxv. 4).

ELDAD — prophesied, with Medad, in the Israelitish camp in the wilderness (Num. xi. 26).

ELEAD—a descendant of Ephraim. Killed in endeavouring to carry away Philistine cattle (I Chron. vii. 21).

ELEASAH—1. A man of Judah (I Chron. ii. 39). 2. A descendant of Jonathan (I Chron. viii. 37).

ELEAZAR—1. The third son of Aaron. Became a priest, and later, chief of the Levites, second only to Aaron himself. He ultimately succeeded Aaron in the office of high priesthood (Ex. vi. 23). 2. A son of Abinadab. Was consecrated as keeper of the ark when it returned from Philistine country (I Sam. vii. 1). 3. One of the priests who acted as musicians at the dedication of the wall of Jerusalem in the time of Nehemiah (Neh. xii. 42).

ELHANAN—son of Jair ; slew Lahmi, Goliath's brother (I Chron. xx. 5).

ELI—the high priest whom the child Samuel served and whom he succeeded in office. Deeply pious but not sufficiently firm with his sons, Hophni and Phinehas. Divine judgment against him and his house was announced by Samuel. When the ark was lost in battle with the Philistines, Eli, now aged 98, fell back from the gate on which he was sitting, and broke his neck. He judged Israel forty years (I Sam. i. 9; iii. 21).

ELIAB—1. Head of the tribe of Zebulun (Num. i. 9). 2. Father of Dathan and Abiram (Num. xvi. 1). 3. David's eldest brother. Tall and kingly, but was not chosen for that office when Samuel came to Bethlehem in fulfilment of God's command. Did not seem able to understand his younger brother (I Sam. xvi. 6). 4. A Gadite who joined David at Ziklag (I Chron. xii. 9).

ELIADA—1. One of Jehoshaphat's chief captains (II Chron.x vii. 17).

ELIADAH-Father of Rezon, who fled from his own country and gave trouble to Solomon (I Kings xi. 23).

ELIAH—1. A Benjamite, son of Jeroham (I Chron. viii. 27). 2. A son of Elam (Ezra x. 26).

ELIAHBA—a Shaalbonite, one of David's mighty men (II Sam. xxiii. 32).

ELIAKIM—1. Son of Melea (Luke iii. 30). 2. Son of Hilkiah. Was placed over Hezekiah's household, and was one of the representatives who parleyed with

Rabshakeh, the representative of King Sennacherib at the siege of Jerusalem (II Kings xviii. 18). 3. One of Josiah's sons (II Kings xxiii. 34). 4. One of Zerubbabel's priests (Neh. xii. 41).

ELIAM—1. Father of Bathsheba (II Sam. xi. 3). 2. One of David's mighty men (? same as 1). One of David's counsellors (II Sam. xxiii. 34). Variant, Ammiel, margin.

ELIASAPH—1. Head of the tribe of Gad, in the wilderness (Num. i. 14). 2. A Levite (Num. iii. 24).

ELIASHIB—1. Head of a priestly course (1 Chron. xxiv. 12). 2. Father of Johanan (Ezra x. 6). 3. The high priest in the time of Nehemiah. Took the lead in rebuilding the sheepgate of Jerusalem (Neh. xii. 10).

ELIATHAH—a musician in the reign of David (I Chron. xxv. 4).

ELIDAD—a prince whom Moses appointed as representative of the tribe of Benjamin (Num. xxxiv. 21).

ELIEL—1. A Gadite associated with David at Ziklag (I Chron. xii. 11). 2. An overseer of the tithes and offerings in the reign of Hezekiah (II Chron. xxxi. 13).

ELIENAI—a Benjamite, son of Shimhi (I Chron. viii. 20).

ELIEZER—1. A man of Damascus. Steward of Abraham's house (Gen. xv. 2). 2. Younger son of Moses (Ex. xviii. 4). 3. A prophet. Son of Dodovah of Mareshah (II Chron. xx. 37). 4. One of Ezra's subordinates (Ezra viii. 16).

ELIHOENAI—a son of Zerahiah (Ezra viii. 4).

ELIHOREPH—a scribe, the elder son of Shisha (I Kings iv. 3).

ELIHU—1. David's eldest brother (I Chron. xxvii. 18) same as Eliab (which see). 2. One of Job's friends (Job xxxii.-xxxvii).

ELIJAH—an early and great Old Testament prophet. A native of Thisbe of Gilead. Appeared before Ahab and predicted a long drought in punishment of Ahab's sin. Went into retirement first at Cherith brook, where he was miraculously fed, then to Sarepta of Sidon, where again he was miraculously sustained. Returned to Carmel, where he challenged and defeated the prophets of Baal. Then he fled to the south for awhile. Returned to perform further witnessing for God. Finally was "translated" to Heaven in a chariot of fire. Was regarded as a type of John the Baptist (I Kings xvii. 1, etc.).

ELIKA—a Harodite; one of David's mighty men (II. Sam. xxiii. 25).

ELIMELECH—husband of Naomi (Ruth i. 1-5).

ELIOENAI—1. A Korhite porter (I Chron. xxvi. 3). 2. A descendant of Simeon (I Chron. iv. 36). 3. El-

dest son of Neraiah (I Chron. iii. 23).

ELIPHAL—one of David's mighty men (I Chron. xi. 35).

ELIPHAZ—1. A son of Esau (Gen. xxxvi. 4). 2. A Temanite. One of Job's friends (Job ii. 11).

ELIPHELEH—a Levite—singer and harper (I Chron. xv. 21).

ELIPHELET—1. A son, born to David (I Chron. iii. 6). 2. A descendant of Jonathan (I Chron. viii. 39). 3. Returned with Ezra from Babylon (Ezra viii. 13).

ELISABETH—wife of Zacharias and mother of John the Baptist. Welcomed Mary as the mother of our Lord (Luke i. 5-45).

ELISHA—succeeded Elijah. One of the great prophets. Born at Abel-meholeh; son of Shaphat. Received Elijah's mantle when that prophet was being " translated." Wrought many miracles, and healed the waters of an unclean spring. Brought condign punishment upon forty-two young lads who called after him. Raised from death the Shunammite's son whose birth he had previously foretold. Cured Naaman's leprosy. Caused an iron axe-head to swim. Revealed to his servant the horses and chariots of God around the mountain when a host of enemies came to take him. He predicted the raising of the siege of Samaria, with consequent plenty. Even after death his remains restored a man miraculously to life (*see* many references from I Kings xix. 16, onwards into II Kings.)

ELISHAH—son of Javan (Gen. x. 4).

ELISHAMA—1. Son of Amihud (Num. i. 10). 2. Son of David (I Chron. iii. 6). 3. Priest sent by Jehoshaphat (II Chron. xvii. 8). 4. Grandfather of the Ishmael who murdered Gedaliah (II Kings xxv. 25).

ELISHAPHAT—a supporter of Jehoida in the revolt against Athaliah (II Chron. xxiii. 1).

ELISHEBA—daughter of Amminadab and wife of Aaron (Ex. vi. 23).

ELIUD—son of Achim (Matt. i. 14-15).

ELIZAPHAN—son of Uzziel (Num. iii. 30).

ELIZUR—prince of the Reubenites in the wilderness (Num. i. 5).

ELKANAH—1. Second son of Korah (Ex. vi. 24). 2. Husband of Hannah and Peninnah (I Sam. i. 1). 3. A dignitary at the court of Ahaz (II Chron. xxviii. 7).

ELMODAM—son of Er, father of Cosam (Luke iii. 28).

ELNAAM—his sons were valiant men in David's army (I Chron. xi. 46).

EL-NATHAN—father of Nehushta, the mother of King Jehoiachin (II Kings xxiv. 8).

ELON—1. A Zebulonite who judged Israel for ten years (Judg. xii. 11). 2. Father-

in-law of Esau (Gen. xxvi. 34).

ELPAAL—a man of Benjamin, son of Hushim (I Chron. viii. 11).

ELUZAI—a supporter of David at Ziklag (I Chron. xii. 5).

ELYMAS—a sorcerer who opposed Paul by seeking to pervert Sergius Paulus in Cyprus. Was stricken with temporary blindness, an act which served to confirm the religious faith of Sergius Paulus (Acts xiii. 6-12).

ELZABAD—a son of Shemaiah, and a porter in David's reign (I Chron. xxvi. 7).

EMMANUEL—the New Testament Greek form of Immanuel, meaning in the Hebrew, "God with us," and applied to Christ (Matt i. 23).

ENOCH—1. the eldest son of Cain (presumably not Cain the "fugitive"—*see* under "Cain,"—but the Cain who builded a city which he named after his son) ; he is shown in the Cainite genealogy (distinct from the Sethite genealogy) as the third in descent from Adam (Gen. iv. f.).

Some hold that the resemblances between the two genealogies warrant the idea that they both rest on a common tradition which is preserved in different forms by early literature. 2. A son of Jared, and father of Methuselah (Gen. v. 18-24). Because of the substitution of the phrase, "And Enoch walked with God, and he was not, for God took him," for the usual formula, "And he died," innumerable speculations have arisen—perhaps justified to some extent by the legends preserved in the apocalyptic *Book of Enoch* (a brief quotation from which occurs in the *Epistle of Jude*, verse 14 ff.).

The "translation" of this patriarch to Heaven, without tasting death, is paralleled in Assyrian mythology by the translation of Sit-Napisti.

ENOS—son of Seth (Gen. iv. 26).

EPÆNETUS—a convert of Achaia (Rom. xvi. 5).

EPAPHRAS—a Colossian Christian who visited Paul in Rome (Col. i. 7).

EPAPHRODITUS—a Christian; sent to Rome as representative of the Philippian church. Became sick so that his life was despaired of, but ultimately recovered. Some suggest that he was the same as Epaphras above, but this is doubtful (Phil. ii. 25-30).

EPHAH—eldest son of Midian. His descendants are referred to as rich in camels and dromedaries (Gen. xxv 4).

EPHAI—a Netophathite who sought protection of Gedaliah, but was afterwards massacred (Jer. xl. 8).

EPHER—1. Second son of Midian (Gen. xxv. 4). 2. A chief man in the half-tribe of Manasseh (I Chron. v. 24).

EPHLAL—a man of Judah; son of Zabad (I Chron. ii. 37).

EPHRAIM—younger son of Joseph; born while Joseph was prime minister of Egypt. In blessing Joseph's sons, Jacob intentionally put his right hand on the head of Ephraim, explaining that Ephraim should become greater than his brother Manasseh. Though only a grandson of Jacob he was treated as though he were a son and regarded as the founder of a tribe (Gen. xlii. 45).

EPHRATHAH—second wife of Caleb (I Chron. ii. 50).

EPHRON—son of Zohar the Hittite (Gen. xxiii. 8).

ER—1. Eldest son of Judah, died through some judgment of God (Gen. xxxviii. 3). 2. Father of Elmodam (Luke iii. 28).

ERAN—son of Shuthelah, and founder of the Eranite family (Num. xxvi. 36).

ERASTUS—a Christian who ministered to Paul (Acts xix. 22).

ERI—a son of Gad and founder of the Erites (Gen. xlvi. 16).

ESARHADDON—third son of Sennacherib, king of Assyria; his father's favourite (II Kings xix. 37).

ESAU—twin brother of Jacob; son of Isaac and Rebekah. Became a skilful hunter. Was robbed both of his birthright and of his blessing by his more sly brother Jacob. He resolved to kill Jacob, but his purpose was frustrated by the brother being sent away to Padan Aram. The two were reconciled later in life. Esau subsequently became the father of the Edomite nation. His second name was Edom (red) from the pottage for which he sold his birthright (Gen. xxv. 25).

ESH-BAAL—a son of King Saul (also called Ishbosheth) (1 Chron. viii. 33; II Sam. ii .8).

ESHBAN—a descendant of Seir the Horonite (Gen. xxxvi. 26).

ESHEK—a Benjamite; brother of Azel (I Chron. viii. 39).

ESHTEMOA—a Maachathite, son of Mered (I Chron. iv. 19).

ESHTON—son of Mehir (I Chron. iv. 11).

ESLI—son of Nagge (Luke iii. 25).

ESTHER—a beautiful maiden brought up at Shushan. Afterwards she succeeded Vashti as Ahasuerus' queen. She was the means of preserving her race from the plot initiated by the wicked Haman . . . (see the whole story in the Book that bears her name).

ETHAN—1. Son of Zerah and grandson of Pharez (I Chron. ii. 6). 2. A Kohathite Levite, son of Zimmah (I Chron. vi. 42).

ETHBAAL—a king of the Sidonians and father of Jezebel (I Kings xvi. 31).

ETHNAN—a man of Judah, son of Helah (I Chron. iv. 7).

ETHNI—a Gershonite Le-

vite, son of Zerah (I
Chron. vi. 41).

EUBULUS—a Roman
Christian who joined Paul
in sending salutations to
Timothy (II Tim. iv. 21).

EUNICE—mother of Timo-
thy (II Tim. i. 5).

EUODIAS—a female Christ-
ian at Philippi who was
apparently at variance
with Syntyche (Phil. iv.
2).

EUTYCHUS—a young man
of Troas who fell through
the open window whilst
Paul was preaching, but
was restored to life by the
Apostle (Acts xx. 9).

EVE—Adam's wife; her
name is assumed by many
to denote "life," "occu-
pation," and therefore
might mean pre-eminently
" motherhood."

In the Bible narrative
which details Eve's deception by the serpent, she
is presented as little more
than a personification of
human life perpetuated by
woman; in the New Testa-
ment St. Paul also appears
to regard Eve in somewhat
the same light.

It is interesting to note
that many argue that the
story of the Fall indicates
a stage of culture wherein
woman was already in the
subordinate position to
man (Gen. iii. ff.).

EVI—one of the five kings
of Midian (Num. xxxi.
8).

EZBAI—father of Naari; one
of David's mighty men
(I Chron. xi. 37).

EZBON—son of Gad (Gen.
xlvi. 16).

EZEKIEL—one of the
greater Jewish prophets.
A son of Buzi, he began
to prophesy in the " fifth
year of his banishment," or
exile, and continued for
not less than 22 years.
Little is known of his
personal history. He pro-
phesied among the exiles
in Babylon during part of
the time that Jeremiah was
prophesying in Judah and
Jerusalem (see his Book,
especially the first chapter.
Variant, Jehezekal, wh. see).

EZER—1. A Horite duke
(Gen. xxxvi. 21). 2. A
son of Ephraim, killed by
Philistines (I Chron. vii,
21). 3. A son of Joshua
who repaired the walls of
Jerusalem (Neh. iii. 19).

EZRA—a priest descended
from Zadok and from
Phinehas. Best known as
a scribe. He is generally
regarded as having much
to do with the arrange-
ment of the Pentateuch
and the general arrange-
ment of the earlier Scrip-
tures. He was apparently
born in Babylon, and
served under the Persian
sovereign Artaxerxes
Longimanus. Was sent to
Judah to lead in the re-
building of the Temple.
A devout and greatly
influential man (see his
Book).

EZRI—a man set over King
David's tillage (I Chron.
xxvii. 26).

F

FELIX—brother of Pallas,
through whose influence

with Nero he was appointed procurator of Judæa ; though touched by Paul's preaching, when forced because of misgovernment to vacate his office, he " left Paul bound "—and himself, too ! (Acts xxiii-xxiv).

FESTUS—procurator of Judæa, following Felix ; from him Paul appealed to Cæsar and was sent to Rome (Acts xxvi. 24 ff.).

FORTUNATUS—one of the messengers between the Church at Corinth and Paul while at Ephesus (Acts xvi. 17).

G

GAAL—a son of Eber, organizer of the revolt against Abimelech on the part of discontented Shechemites (Judg. ix. 26 ff.).

GABBAI—a Benjamite, active in post-exilic affairs (Neh. xi. 8).

GABRIEL—one of the seven archangels, especially associated with Michael (Dan. viii. 15). In the Old Testament he is seen as the interpreter of visions and prophecies—in the New Testament as ambassador and announcer. *Equivalents* to the seven archangels of the Jews are found in the angelologies of Babylonia and Persia.

GAD—1. Son of Jacob and Zilpah (Gen. xxx. 9 ff.). 2. A prophet associated on several occasions with David (I Sam. xxii. 5). 3. A Canaanitish deity (Gen. xxx. 11).

GADARENES—inhabitants of Gadara (Mark v. 1). *Variant*, Gergesenes.

GADDI—a Manassite spy (Num. xiii. 11).

GADDIEL—a Zebulunite spy (Num. xiii. 10).

GADI—father of King Menaham (II Kings xv. 14).

GAHAM—son of Nahor (Gen. xxii. 24).

GAHAR—head of a family of Nathinim (Ezra ii. 47).

GAIUS—1. One of Paul's travelling companions (Acts xix. 29). 2. Paul's host at Corinth, probably one of his converts (I Cor. i. 14 and Rom. xvi. 23). 3. Person to whom III John is addressed (III John i).

GALAL—name of two post-exilic Levites (I Chron. ix. 15 and ix. 16).

GALLIO—elder brother of Seneca, proconsul of Achaia during Paul's first visit to Corinth—a man of fine character in spite of the slur erroneously attached to his judicial pronouncement (Acts xviii. 12 ff.).

GAMALIEL—1. Son of Pedahzur and prince of Manasseh (Num. i. 10). 2. A great rabbi, at the feet of whom Paul studied (Acts xxii. 3).

GAMMADIMS—evidently refers to a people near Tyre, but whose identity is doubtful (Ezek. xxvii. 11).

GAMUL—ancestral head of the 22nd course of priests (I Chron. xxiv. 17).

GAREB—one of David's " thirty " chiefs (II. Sam. xxiii. 38).

GASHMU—*see* Geshem.

GATAM—son of Eliphaz and a "duke" (i.e. chief) of Edom (Gen. xxxvi. 11, 16).

GAZEZ—names of two Calebites (1 Chron. ii. 46).

GAZZAM—a sub-division of the Nethinim (Ezra ii. 48).

GEBER—one of twelve officers of Solomon in charge of his commissariat (I Kings iv. 19).

GEDALIAH—1. Son of Ahikam; probably grandson of Shaphan (II Kings xxv. 22 f.). 2. Son of Jeduthun (I Chron. xxv. 3, 9). 3. A priest who married a "strange" woman (Ezra x. 18). 4. Son of Pashhur (Jer. xxxviii. 1). 5. Son of Hezekiah (Zeph. i. 1).

GEDOR—1. Ancestor of Saul (I Chron. viii. 31). 2. Name of two Judahite families (I Chron. iv. 4, 18).

GEHAZI—servant of the prophet Elisha (II Kings iv. ff.).

GEMALLI—father of one of the twelve spies (Num. xiii. 12).

GEMARIAH—1. "Son of Shaphan the scribe" (Jer. xxxvi. 10 ff.). 2. Son of Hilkiah (Jer. xxix. 3).

GENUBATH—son of Hadad (I Kings xi. 20).

GERA—one of the ancient clans of Benjamin (Gen. xlvi. 21).

GERSHOM—1. Son of Levi, head of a priestly family of the Gershonites (I Chron. vi. 16 ff.). *Variant,* Gershon. 2 Eldest son of Moses (Ex. ii. 22). 3.

Descendant of Phinehas (Ezra viii. 2).

GERSHONITES — descendants of Gershon (Num. iii. 21) *see* also Gershom).

GESHAM—descendant of Caleb (I Chron. ii. 47).

GESHEM—an opponent of Nehemiah during the rebuilding of the wall of Jerusalem (Neh. ii. 19). *Variant,* Gashmu.

GESHURITES—an Aramean tribe (Josh. xiii. 11.)

GETHER—one of " the sons of Aram " (Gen. x. 23).

GEUEL—one of the twelve spies (Num. xiii. 15).

GEZRITES—a people raided by David (I Sam. xxvii. 8). *Variant,* Gerzites—*margin.*

GIDDALTI—son of Heman and a temple musician (I Chron. xxv. 4).

GIDDEL—1. Head of a family of Nethinim (Ezra ii. 47). 2. Head of one of the sub-divisions of Solomon's servants (Ezra ii. 56).

GIDEON—son of Joash, a great military leader. (Judg. vi. 11). *Variants,* Jerubbaal, Jerubbesheth.

GIDEONI—father of Abidan (Num. i. 11).

GILALAI—a post-exilic Levite (Neh. xii. 36).

GILEAD—1. Son of Machir (Num. xxvi. 29). 2. Gadite son of Michael (I Chron. v. 14). 3. Father of Jephthah (Judg. xi. 1).

GINATH—father of Tibni (I Kings xvi. 21 f.).

GINNETHON—a post-exilic priest (Neh. x. 6). *Variant,* Ginnetho.

GIRGASITE—one of the Canaanite tribes (Gen. x. 16). *Variant*, Girgashites.

GISPA—probably an overseer of the Nethinim (Neh. xi. 21).

GOD—one of the names by which we designate the Eternal, Infinite, Incomprehensible Being, the Creator of all things; Ruler of all nations as well as of the Universe—Omnipresent (occupying all space), Omnipotent (almighty in power), Omniscient (possessing all knowledge) (Gen. i. ff.).

The origin of the word " GOD " is uncertain, but is regarded by some as probably derived from Teutonic sources, and would in such case appear to have a pagan history.

The Hebrews assigned to God the name " Jehovah " (Yahweh), and held this name in such profound veneration that they never pronounced it, but instead of it made use of that of " Adonai " (signifying, " My Lords "—in the plural number).

We may conveniently group the principal Old Testament names of God, thus—

1. ELOHIM (a plural word of doubtful origin and meaning—thought to denote " The Fulness of God ").

2. EL (of doubtful meaning, but interpreted by many as " The Strong One ").

3. EL-SHADDAI (original meaning uncertain; may signify, " One Who is Self-sufficient ").

4. EL-ELYON, or EL-SABAOTH (signifying " The Most High " and " The God of Hosts," respectively).

5. ADONAI (" My Lords " —used sometimes in the plural number in relation to heathen gods; but when applied to GOD, it uses a *singular* verb).

6. JEHOVAH (Yahweh)— the usual name for GOD in post-Mosaic times, but perhaps a pre-historic name meaning— " Self-Existent ").

Here also may be set down the names given to GOD by the principal nations of the world :

1. Arabians . . Alla.
2. Assyrians . . Adad.
3. Egyptians . . Thoth.
4. French . . . . Dieu.
5. Germans . . Gott.
6. Grecians . . . Theos.
7. Italians . . . Idio.
8. Latins . . . . Deus.
9. Persians . . . Eoru (also Sire).
10. Spaniards Dios.

GOD is, it goes without saying, the fundamental subject of the Bible—throughout the sacred volume His existence is assumed ; it opens, as it closes, by showing Him as " Father " and " Friend." There is no need in this particular place to deal with the story of God's " Self-revelation," to show how the world gradually acquired the knowledge of God which we now possess; it will suffice present purposes if we summarize briefly some of the more important conceptions of GOD, such as the—

1. PRE-MOSAIC CONCEPTIONS OF GOD.—The Old Testament recognizes affinities with earlier conceptions—for instance, we find that the God of whom Moses teaches is " the God of their fathers " (*Exodus* iii. 4, 15 ; & vi. 3) ; that before Jehovah is revealed to Moses He has been already known to other tribes (*Exodus* iii. 18)—and, further, the knowledge recently gained of Babylonian and Egyptian religions would tend to prove that some races had, in spite of their "many gods," attained to something somewhat more lofty than mere " polytheism." Traces of some of the primitive forms of religion may be discerned in the pre-Mosaic religious customs and ceremonies of Israel, " Totemism " (belief in the blood relationship of a tribe) ; " Animism " (belief in the survival of the spirits of dead relatives) ; " Ancestor-worship " (with its mourning, hair-cutting, sackcloth, reverence for the dead, etc.).

2. POST-MOSAIC CONCEPTIONS OF GOD.—The worship of Jehovah was begun under Moses amid such beliefs and practices, but three things their prophets make clear ; (i.) Jehovah is alone God ; (ii.) He loathes idolatry ; (iii.) His character is altogether righteous.

Thus during the ages, through many changes— racial, political, economic, intellectual, moral—the light of God's " Self-revelation " developed, until it culminated in a pure monotheism (the doctrine that there is but *one* God), though Israel for long retained the habit of thinking of their God as if He were a human being (anthropomorphism)—leading to the expectation of a superhuman King-Messiah.

3. THE CHRISTIAN CONCEPTION OF GOD. Here, due to the coming of Jesus Christ, " the Light of the world "—" the way, the truth, and the life "—we are in a new world with a new religion. We do not have to grope up to God through lower grades of knowledge, but begin with Christ, who came to reveal God fully as " Father " and " Friend." According to the Christian conception, " God is the Personal Spirit, perfectly good, who in holy love creates, sustains and orders all things." As to His *nature*—God is a Personal Spirit ; a Self-conscious, Self-directing Intelligence. In regard to *character*—God is perfectly good without qualification ; His *relation* to all other existence is this : " He creates all, sustains all, orders all, from the motive of Holy Love." The Christian conception of God excels all other. To the Greeks, Theos was a God of *Beauty* ; to the

Romans, Deus was a God of *Power*; to the Jews, Jehovah was a God of *Law*; but Christians, through the revelation of Jesus Christ, know the Father as the God of *Love*. The ground of their faith is : " God so loved the world, that He gave His only begotten Son, that whosoever believeth in Him should not perish, but have everlasting life."

One last thing to be noted : The New Testament does not seek to present an elaborated theory or doctrine of the Trinity ; but while retaining all the highest Old Testament conceptions of God, it gives us to behold the living picture of a little community of believers to whom has come the very indwelling of the Triune God, and in that holy fellowship they enjoy the revelation of God as *Father*, Jesus Christ as *Brother*, and Holy Spirit as *Friend*— three modes of Self-unveiling of the one true God.

GOG—1. A name linked with Magog (Ezek. xxxviii ff.). 2. Descendant of Reuben (I Chron. v. 4).

GOLIATH—a Philistine giant (I Sam. xvii. 4 ff.).

GOMER—1. Son of Japheth (Gen. x. 2 f.). 2. Wife of Hosea (Hos. i. 3).

H

HAAHASHTARI—a son of Ashur ; the latter was termed the " father of Tekoa " (1 Chron. iv. 6).

HABAIAH—father of certain Jews who wrongly claimed sacerdotal descent (Ezra ii. 61).

HABAKKUK—one of the minor prophets. Nothing is known of his life ; he is known only through his Book (which *see*).

HABAZINIAH—a Rechabite, and father of a certain Jeremiah (Jer. xxxv. 3).

HACHALIAH—the father of Nehemiah (Neh. i. 1).

HACHMONI—father of Jehiel (I Chron. xxvii. 32).

HADAD—1. Eighth son of Ishmael (Gen. xxv. 15). 2. The name of two kings of Edom (Gen. xxxvi. 35 ; I Chron. i. 50). 3. An Edomite prince who escaped the sword of Joab and was treated kindly by Pharaoh in Egypt. In later years patriotism drove him back to his own land (I Kings xi. 14).

HADADEZER—a king of Zobah in Syria ; was defeated on more than one occasion by David (II Sam. viii. 3).

HADASSAH—afterwards Queen Esther (Esther ii. 7).

HADLAI—father of Amasa (II Chron. xxviii. 12).

HAGABAH—founder of a family of Nethinim (Ezra ii. 45).

HAGAR—servant of Sarah, Abraham's wife ; was the mother of Ishmael and was sent forth from the camp with her son toward the south (Gen. xxi. 12 f.).

HAGGAI—a minor prophet; contemporary with Zechariah. Nothing is known of him except what may be

gathered from his Book (which *see*).

HAGGERI—father of Mibhar (I Chron. xi. 38).

HAGGI—son of Gad (Gen. xlvi. 16).

HAKKATAN—father of Johanan (Ezra viii. 12).

HAKKOZ—chief of the seventh course of the priesthood appointed by David (I Chron. xxiv. 10).

HAKUPHA—founder of a family of Nethinim (Ezra ii. 51).

HALOHESH—father of Shallum (Neh. iii. 12).

HAM—youngest son of Noah ; behaved very undutifully to his father (Gen. v. 32).

HAMAN—a high official at the court of King Ahasuerus, who sought to appease his injured pride by a wholesale massacre of the Jews. He was thwarted through Esther's strategy, and was executed on the gallows he had prepared for Mordecai (Esther iii. 1).

HAMMEDATHA—father of Haman (Esther iii. 1).

HAMMOLEKETH—a Manassite, sister of Gilead (I Chron. vii. 18).

HAMOR—father of Shechem (Gen. xxxiii. 20).

HAMUEL—eldest son of Mishma (I Chron. iv. 26).

HAMUTAL—daughter of Jeremiah of Libnah. Wife of King Josiah (II Kings xxiii. 31).

HANAMEEL—son of Shallum (Jer. xxxii. 7).

HANAN—1. One of David's mighty men (I Chron. xi. 43). 2. Youngest son of Azel (I Chron. viii. 38). 3. Founder of a family of Nethinim (Ezra ii. 46). 4. A Jew, appointed as a treasurer by Nehemiah (Neh. xiii. 13).

HANANI—1. Father of the prophet Jehu (I Kings xvi. 1). 2. Brother of Nehemiah (Neh. i. 2). 3. Priestly son of Immer (Ezra x. 20). 4. A musician under Nehemiah (Neh. xii. 36).

HANANIAH—1. Son of Heman (I Chron. xxv. 4). 2. One of King Uzziah's captains (II Chron. xxvi. 11). 3. Father of a certain Zedekiah (Jer. xxxvi. 12). 4. A Gibeonite, son of Azur (Jer. xxviii. 1-17). 5. Father of Shelemiah (Jer. xxxvii. 13). 6. The Hebrew name of Shadrach (Dan. i. 6). 7. A son of Zerubbabel (I Chron. iii. 19). 8. Governor of the castle, under Nehemiah (Neh. vii. 2).

HANNAH—wife of Elkanah, and mother of Samuel (I Sam. i. 1-28).

HANNIEL—prince of the Manassites during later wilderness wanderings (Num. xxxiv. 23).

HANOCH—a descendant of Abraham (Gen. xxv. 4). 2. Eldest son of Reuben (Gen. xlvi. 9).

HANUN—1. A king of the Ammonites who grossly illtreated David's ambassadors, whom he suspected of treachery (II Sam. x. 1). 2. A Jew who repaired the valley gate, under Nehemiah (Neh. iii. 13).

HARAN—youngest son of

Terah, and brother of Abraham (Gen. xi. 29).

HARBONA—one of the chamberlains of Ahasuerus (Esther i. 10).

HAREPH—a son of Caleb (I Chron. ii. 51).

HARHAIAH—father of Uzziel the goldsmith (Neh. iii. 8).

HARHAS—an ancestor of Shallum (II Kings xxii. 14)

HARHUR—founder of a family of Nethinim (Ezra ii. 51).

HARIM—1. Head of the third course of the priesthood (I Chron. xxiv. 8). 2. Founder of a family who returned with Zerubbabel (Ezra ii. 32).

HARIPH—founder of a family who returned with Zerubbabel (Neh. vii. 24).

HARNEPHER—son of Zophar (I Chron. vii. 36).

HAROEH—eldest son of Shobal (I Chron. ii. 52).

HARSHA—founder of a family of Nethinim (Ezra ii. 52).

HARUM—a man of Judah, father of Aharhel (I Chron. iv. 8).

HARUMAPH—father of Jedaiah (Neh. iii. 10).

HARUZ—father of King Manasseh's wife, Meshullemeth (II Kings xxi. 19).

HASADIAH—fourth son of Zerubbabel (I Chron. iii. 20).

HASENUAH—a Benjamite; father of Hodaviah (I Chron. ix. 7).

HASHABIAH—there are thirteen persons of this name mentioned in the Bible. They are of minor importance, and the following are the references to them : I Chron. vi. 45 ; I Chron. ix. 14 ; I Chron. xxv. 3 ; I Chron. xxvi. 30 ; I Chron. xxvii. 17 ; II Chron. xxxv. 9 ; Ezra viii. 19 ; Ezra viii. 24 ; Neh. iii. 17 ; Neh. x. 11 ; Neh. xi. 15 ; Neh. xi. 22 ; Neh. xii. 21.

HASHABNAH—one who, with Nehemiah, sealed the covenant (Neh. x. 25).

HASHBADANA—a supporter of Ezra (Neh. viii. 4).

HASHEM—a " Gizronite " ; his sons were among David's mighty men (I Chron. xi. 34).

HASHUB—a Jew who repaired part of the wall under Nehemiah (Neh. iii. 23).

HASHUBAH—third son of Zerubbabel (I Chron. iii. 20).

HASHUM—founder of a family of returned exiles under Zerubbabel (Ezra ii. 19).

HASRAH—father of Tickvath (II Chron. xxxiv. 22).

HASSENAAH—a Jew whose son rebuilt the fish gate of Jerusalem under Nehemiah (Neh. iii. 3).

HASUPHA—founder of a family of Nethinim (Ezra ii. 43).

HATACH—a chamberlain of King Ahasuerus (Esther iv. 5).

HATHATH—a son of Othniel (I Chron. iv. 13).

HATIPHA—founder of a family of Nethinim (Ezra ii. 54).

HATITA—a porter under Zerubbabel (Ezra ii. 42).

HATTIL—one of Solomon's servants (Ezra ii. 57).

HATTUSH—a son of Shemiah (I Chron. iii. 22).

HAZAEL—a Syrian courtier, annointed by Elijah as king over Syria (I Kings xi . 17).

HAZAIAH—a descendant of Shelah (Neh. xi. 5).

HAZARMARVETH—a son of Joktan (Gen. x. 26).

HAZELELPONI—a woman of Judah (I Chron. iv. 3).

HAZIEL—a Gershonite Levite; son of Shimei (I Chron. xxiii. 9).

HEBER—1. Grandson of Asher (Gen. xlvi. 17). 2. A Kenite, son of Hobab (Judg. iv. 11-24). 3. A Gadite, dwelling in Bashan (I Chron. v. 13).

HEGE—one of King Ahasuerus' chamberlains (Esther ii. 3).

HELAH—wife of Ashur (I Chron. iv. 5).

HELDAI—one of David's captains (I Chron. xxvii. 15).

H E L E D—one of David's mighty men (I Chron. xi. 30).

HELEK—a son of Gilead (Num. xxvi. 30).

HELEM—an Asherite, brother of Shamer (I Chron. vii. 35).

HELEZ—one of David's mighty men (II Sam. xxiii. 26).

HELKAI—a priest of Meraioth (Neh. xii. 15).

HELON—a man of Zebulun (Num. i. 9).

HEMAN—1. A wise man of Solomon's reign (I Kings iv. 31). 2. A singer of David's reign (I Chron. vi. 33).

HEMATH—" father " of the house of Rechab (I Chron. ii. 55).

HEN—a son of Zephaniah (Zech. vi. 14).

HENADAD—founder of a Levitical family (Ezra iii. 9).

HEPHER—son of Gilead (Num. xxvi. 32).

HEPHZIBAH—mother of King Manasseh (II Kings xxi. 1).

HERMAS—a Christian at Rome to whom Paul sent greetings (Rom. xvi. 14).

HERMES—1. A Christian at Rome to whom Paul sent greetings (Rom. xvi. 14). 2. The name of the Greek god corresponding to the Roman Mercury (Acts xiv. 12).

HERMOGENES—an early Christian who became apostate (II Tim. i. 15).

H E R O D—1. Herod the Great, son of Antipas, born about 73 B.C. ; became ruler of Galilee 48 B.C. Rebuilt the temple at Jerusalem. Was responsible for the slaughter of the innocents (Matt. ii. 1–19). 2. Herod the Tetrarch. Was responsible for the murder of John the Baptist (Matt. xiv. 1-13). 3. "Herod the king" is the same as Agrippa I (which see).

HERODIAS—being divorced from her husband, she became the guilty wife of Herod the Tetrarch and shared the responsibility for John the Baptist's death (see reference above).

HETH—second son of Canaan (Gen. x. 15).

HEZEKI—a Benjamite, son of Elpaal (I Chron. viii. 17).

HEZEKIAH—son of Ahaz, whom he succeeded ; was a devoted follower of Jehovah, and did much to reform the life of his people. Was on the throne during the marvellous deliverance of his people from the hand of Sennacherib, and owed much of his power to the guidance of the prophet Isaiah. Was granted an extension of life when he had been " sick unto death " (*see* II. Chron. xxix. 1 to xxxii. 33).

H E Z I O N—grandfather of Ben-hadad the king of Syria (I Kings xv. 18).

HEZIR—one of the chiefs who sealed the covenant with Nehemiah (Neh. x. 20).

HEZRAI—a Carmelite ; one of David's mighty men (II Sam. xxiii. 35).

HEZRON—third son of Reuben (Gen. xlvi. 9) ; father of Ashur (1 Chron. ii. 24).

HIDDAI—one of David's heroes from the brooks of Gaash (II Sam. xxiii. 30).

HIEL—a native of Bethel, who tried to rebuild Jericho, and shared the consequent curse (I Kings xvi. 34).

HILLEL—father of Abson (Judg. xii. 13).

HIRAH—an Adullamite, a friend of Judah (Gen. xxxviii. 1).

HIRAM—a king of Tyre and Sidon who sent cedar trees, etc., to David for the temple (II Sam. v. 11). Nearly 30 years later he was still reigning and sent congratulations to Solomon (I Kings v. 1 ff.).

HIZKIAH—an ancestor of Zephaniah (Zeph. i. 1).

HOBAB—a son of Raguel (the father-in-law of Moses). Was asked to accompany the Israelites on their journey, but refused (Num. x. 29-32).

HOD—son of Zophah (I Chron. vii. 37).

HODAIAH—a son of Elioenai (I Chron. iii. 24).

H O D A V I A H—a Levite, founder of a family (Ezra ii. 40).

HODESH—wife of the Benjamite Shaharaim (I Chron. viii. 9).

HODIJAH—one of those employed by Ezra to explain the law (Neh. viii. 7).

HOGLAH—third daughter of Zelophehad (Num. xxvi. 33).

HOHAM—king of Hebron, who became leagued with Joshua (Josh. x. 3).

HOMAM—younger son of Lotan (I Chron. i. 39).

HOPHNI—elder son of Eli , showed himself unworthy of the sacred office of the priesthood ; perished in the war with the Philistines in the course of which the Ark was lost (I Sam. ii. 34).

HORAM—a king of Gezer, slain by Joshua (Josh. x. 33).

HORI—a son of Lotan (Gen. xxxvi. 22).

HOSAH—a porter in the time of David (I Chron. xvi. 38).

HOSEA—a prophet who prophesied during the reigns of Uzziah, Jotham, Ahaz and Hezekiah, kings of Judah, and Jeroboam II of Israel. His book is largely occupied with the working out of his message along what appear to be the lines of his own experience of an unfaithful wife (*see* the Book of Hosea).

HOSHAIAH—father of Jezaniah (Jer. xlii. 1).

HOSHEA—1. Another name for Joshua. *Variant*, Oshea. 2. A son of Elah who conspired against and succeeded Pekah, king of Israel, slaying that monarch. He did evil in the sight of God, but was better in some respects than others in his line of sovereignty (II Kings xv. 30).

HOTHAN—an Areorite, two of whose sons were among David's mighty men. (I Chron. xi. 44).

HOTHIR—son of Heman, David's seer and singer (I Chron. xxv. 4).

HUL—second son of Aram (Gen. x. 23).

HULDAH—a prophetess who lived in the college at Jerusalem (II Kings xxii. 14).

HUPHAM—a son of Benjamin (Num. xxvi. 39).

HUR—1. The man who supported Moses' arms in prayer, in company with Aaron. He was also associated with Aaron in the government of the Israelites while Moses was in the mount (Ex. xvii. 10-12). 2. Grandfather of

Bezaleel (Ex. xxxi. 2). 3. A king of Midian (Num. xxxi. 8).

HURAI—one of David's mighty men (I Chron. xi. 32).

HURI—a Gadite ; father of Abihail (I Chron. v. 14).

HUSHAI—an Archite, a leading counsellor of David (II Sam. xv. 32).

HUSHAM—a man of Temani who succeeded Jobab as king of Edom (Gen. xxxvi. 34).

HUZ—*see* Uz.

HYMENÆUS—made shipwreck of his faith and was excommunicated by Paul (I Tim. i. 20).

I

IBHAR—one of King David's sons (II Sam. v. 15).

IBNEIAH—son of Jeroboam (I Chron. ix. 8).

IBNIJAH—a Benjamite, father of Reuel (I Chron. ix. 8).

IBSAM (Jibsam)—son of Tola (I Chron. vii. 2).

IBZAN—a judge who ruled over Israel for seven years (Judg. xii. 8-10).

ICHABOD—a name meaning " the glory has departed," and given to the son of Phinehas when the ark had been captured (I Sam. iv. 21).

IDDO—(spelt variously in Hebrew.) 1. A Levite, descendant of Gershom (I Chron. vi. 21). 2. A seer who published a book of genealogies connected with the reigns of Solomon and Rehoboam (II Chron. ix. 29). 3. Chief of the half-tribe of Manasseh in David's reign (1 Chron. xxvii.

21). 4. Grandfather of the prophet Zechariah (Zech. i. 1).

IGAL—1. Spy, sent out by the tribe of Issachar to view Canaan (Num. xiii. 7). 2. One of David's mighty men (II Sam. xxiii. 36). 3. *Variant*, Igeal—a son of Shemaiah (I Chron. iii. 22).

IGDALIAH—a " man of God " in Jeremiah's time (Jer. xxxv. 4).

IKKESH—a Tekoite (II Sam. xxiii. 26).

ILAI—one of David's mighty men (I Chron. xi. 29).

IMLA—the father of the prophet Micaiah (I Kings xxii. 8).

IMMANUEL (same as EM-MANUEL)—a name uttered by the prophet Isaiah and generally applied to Christ. The name means " God with us " (Isaiah vii. 14 ; Matt. i. 23).

IMMER—father of Passhur (Jer. xx. 1).

IMNA—an Asherite (I Chron. vii. 35).

IMRAH— an Asherite (I Chron. vii. 36).

IMRI—son of Bani (I Chron. ix. 4).

IPHEDEIAH—son of Shashak (I Chron. viii. 25).

IRA—one of David's mighty men (II Sam. xxiii. 26).

IRAD—grandson of Cain (Gen. iv. 18).

IRAM—a duke of Edom (Gen. xxxvi. 43).

IRI—grandson of Benjamin (I Chron. vii. 7, 12).

IRIJAH—a Benjamite captain in charge of the gates of Jerusalem in Jeremiah's time (Jer. xxxvii. 13).

IRU—eldest son of Caleb (I Chron. iv. 15).

ISAIAH—perhaps the greatest of all Old Testament prophets. He was the son of Amoz, and prophesied in Judah during the reigns of Uzziah, Jotham, Ahaz and Hezekiah. During a long life he kept faithful to Jehovah and raised the prophetic office to that of statesman. He faced much opposition during his earlier years, but when the crisis came under Sennacherib, he guided the state into a miraculous delivery. Hezekiah repeatedly sought his guidance. The earlier half of the book which bears his name is generally regarded as his work (*see* his Book, especially Chapter VI, for his story).

ISCAH—the sister of Milcah (Gen. xi. 29).

ISCARIOT—part of the name of Judas Iscariot ; the word means " man of Kerioth," and Judas was so called to distinguish him from the other apostle Jude, or Hudas (Matt. x. 4).

ISHBAH—son of a woman called Ezra (I Chron. iv. 17).

ISHBAK—a son of Abraham by Keturah (Gen. xxv. 2).

ISHBI-BENOB—a Philistine giant who sought to kill David, but who was himself killed by Abishai (II Sam. xxi. 16).

ISH-BOSHETH—one of Saul's younger sons, also called Eshbaal. Ishbosheth means " man of shame." He reigned over Judah for a time and sought wider rule, but eventually suffered many defeats, and was ultimately slain, thus bringing to an end the dynasty of Solomon (II Sam. ii. 8-10).

ISHHOD—a Manassite (I Chron. vii. 18).

ISHI—1. Eldest son of Appaim (I Chron. ii. 31). 2. Descendant of Caleb (I Chron. iv. 20). 3. One of the heads of the Manasseh half-tribe (I Chron. v. 24).

ISHIJAH—son of Harim (Ezra x. 31).

ISHMA—a man of Judah (I Chron. iv. 3).

ISHMAEL—eldest son of Abraham, his mother was Hagar, Sarah's handmaid. He accompanied his mother when she was sent away from Abraham's household and became founder of the Ishmaelites (Gen. xvi. 1-14). Other lesser known Ishmaels are : 1. Third son of Azel (I Chron. viii. 38). 2. Father of Zebadiah (II Chron. xix. 11). 3. Son of Jehohanan (II Chron. xxiii. 1). 4. A son of Nethaniah, who belonged to the seed-royal of Judah (II Kings xxv. 25). 5. A son of Passhur (Ezra x. 22).

ISHMAIAH—1. A Gibeonite who joined David at Ziklag (I Chron. xii. 4). 2. Son of Obadiah (I Chron. xxvii. 19).

ISHMERAI—a Benjamite, son of Elpaal (I Chron. viii. 18).

ISHOD—a Manassite (I Chron. vii. 18).

ISHPAN—son of Shashak (I Chron. viii. 22).

ISHUAH—son of Asher (Gen. xlvi. 17).

ISMACHIAH—an overseer of the temple during Hezekiah's reign (II Chron. xxxi. 13).

ISPAH—son of Beriah (I Chron. viii. 16).

ISRAEL—the name given to Jacob by the angel with whom he wrestled at the Jabok ford (Gen. xxxii. 28) (see also " Jacob ").

ISSACHAR—ninth son of Jacob (Gen. xxx. 18).

ITHAMAR — the youngest son of Aaron (Ex. vi. 23).

ITHIEL—father of Maaseiah (Neh. xi. 7).

ITHMAH—a Moabite, one of David's heroes (I Chron. xi. 46).

ITHRA—an Israelite who married Abigail (II Sam. xvii. 25).

ITHRAN—tenth son of Zophah (I Chron. vii. 37).

ITHREAM—sixth son born to King David at Hebron (II Sam. iii. 5).

ITTAI—one of David's mighty men (II Sam. xxiii. 29).

IZHAR—father of Korah, the rebel (Ex. vi. 18).

IZRAHIAH—a man of Issachar ; son of Uzzi (I Chron. vii. 3) (see Jezrahiah).

IZRI—a Levite chosen by lot to be head of the fourth course for the musical service of the sanctuary (I Chron. xxv. 11).

J

JAAKAN—an Edomite clan

(Deut. x. 6). *Variants,* Jakan, Akan.

JAAKOBAH—a princely head of a Simeonite family (I Chron. iv. 36).

JAALA—ancestral head of a family who returned with Zerubbabel (Neh. vii. 58). *Variant,* Jaalah.

JAALAM—son of Esau (Gen. xxxvi. 5).

JAANAI—a Gadite chief (I Chron. v. 12).

JAARE-OREGIM—a name of uncertain identity (cf. II Sam. xxi. 19 and I Chron. xx. 5).

JAASAU—one of those who had married a foreign wife (Ezra x. 37).

JAASIEL—one of David's heroes (I. Chron. xxvii. 21). Probably identical with Jasiel the Mesobaite (I Chron. xi. 47).

JAAZANIAH—1. A military commander who gave allegiance to Gedaliah (II Kings xxv. 23). *Variant,* Jezaniah. 2. A Rechabite chief (Jer. xxxv. 3). 3. Son of Shaphan (Ezek. viii. 11). 4. Son of Azur (Ezek. xi. 1).

JAAZIAH—son of Merari (I Chron. xxiv. 26).

JAAZIEL—a Levite musician (I Chron. xv. 18). *Variant,* Aziel.

JABAL—son of Lamech, an early nomad (Gen. iv. 20).

JABESH—father of Shallum a usurper of the kingdom of Israel (II Kings xv. 10).

JABEZ—a noted head of a family of Judah (I Chron. iv. 9 f.).

JABIN—name of two kings of Hazor, probably identi-

cal (Josh. xi. 1 ; Judg. iv. 2. ff.).

JACAN—chief of a Gadite family (I Chron. v. 13).

JACHIN—1. Son of Simeon (Gen. xlvi. 10). *Variant,* Jarib (I Chron. iv. 24). 2. Ancestral head of a priestly family (I Chron. xxiv. 17).

JACOB—1. Son of Isaac and Rebekah, who figures in the great patriarchal drama with his brothers Esau —probably an idealized cluster of tribal traditions having a religious origin (Gen. xxv. ff.). 2. Father of Joseph (Matt. i. 5).

JADA—a Jerahmeelite tribe (I Chron. ii. 28).

JADDUA—1. A post-exilic chief (Neh. x. 21). 2. A chief priest (Neh. xii. 11).

JADON—a Meronothite who assisted in rebuilding the wall of Jerusalem (Neh. ii. 7).

JAEL—wife of Heber, the Kenite, who treacherously slew Sisera (Judg. iv. 11).

JAH—a shortened form for " Jehovah " (Psalms lxviii. 4.) (*see* God).

JAHATH—1. A clan of Judah (I Chron. iv. 2). 2. Grandson of Levi (I Chron. vi. 20). 3. A Kohathite Levite (I Chron. xxiv. 22). 4. A Merarite Levite (II Chron. xxxiv. 12).

JAHAZIAH—son of Tikvah, represented as helping Ezra (Ezra x. 15).

JAHAZIEL—1. One of the heroes who joined David at Ziklag (I Chron. xii. 4). 2. A priest and trumpeter (I Chron. xvi. 6). 3. A Kohathite Levite

(I Chron. xxiii. 19). 4. An Asaphite Levite (II Chron. xx. 14). 5. Ancestor of a post-exilic family (Ezra viii. 5).

JAHDAI—a Calebite (I Chron. ii. 47).

JAHDIEL—a Manassite chief (I Chron. v. 24.).

JAHDO—a Gadite (I Chron. v. 14).

JAHLEEL—son of Zebulun (Gen. xlvi. 14).

JAHMAI—a man or clan of Issachar (I Chron. vii. 2).

JAHZEEL—head of a clan of Naphtali (Gen. xlvi. 24). *Variant,* Jahziel.

JAHZERAH—a priest (I Chron. ix. 12). *Variant,* Ahasai.

JAHZIEL—*see* Jahzeel.

JAIR—1. A descendant of Manasseh (Num. xxxii. 41). 2. The father of Mordecai (Esther ii. 5). The father of Elhanan (I Chron. xx. 5).

JAIRUS—a synagogue ruler whose daughter Jesus raised from the dead (Mark v. 22).

JAKEH—father of Agur (Prov. xxx. 1).

JAKIM—1. A descendant of Benjamin (I Chron. viii. 19). 2. A priest (I Chron. xxiv. 12).

JALON—a Calebite (I Chron. iv. 17).

JAMBRES—*see* Jannes and Jambres.

JAMES—1. Son of Zebedee (Mark i. 19). 2. Son of Alphæus (Mark iii. 18). 3. The brother of our Lord (Gal. i. 19). 4. Brother of Judas (Luke vi. 16)? *Confused identity.*

JAMIN—1. Ancestor of a clan of Simeon (Gen. xlvi. 10). 2. Ancestor of a family of Judah (I Chron. ii. 27). 3. A priest (Neh. viii. 7).

JAMLECH—a Simeonite chief (I Chron. iv. 34).

JANNA—an ancestor of Jesus (Luke iii. 24).

JANNES and JAMBRES—Egyptian magicians who opposed Moses (Ex. vii. 11 ; II Tim. iii. 8).

JAPHET—a son of Noah (Gen. ix. 27).

JAPHIA—1. A King of Lachish (Josh. x. 3). 2. A Son of David (II Sam. v. 15).

JAPHLET—an Asherite chief (I Chron. vii. 32 f.).

JARAH—one of Saul's descendants (I Chron. ix. 42). *Variant,* Jehoadah.

JAREB—an Assyrian king (Hos. v. 13).

JARED—1. Father of Enoch (Gen. v. 15). 2. A Judahite (I Chron. iv. 18).

JARESHIAH—one of Benjamin's descendants (I Chron. vii. 27).

JARHA—an Egyptian slave. who married the daughter of Sheshan (I Chron. ii. 34 f.).

JARIB—1. The founder of a Simeonite family (I Chron. iv. 24). *Variant,* Jachin. 2. One of Ezra's chief men (Ezra viii. 16). 3. A priest (Ezra x. 18).

JAROAH—a Gadite (I. Chron. v. 14).

JASHEN—" sons of Jashen" are included in list of David's heroes (II Sam. xxiii. 32). *Equivalent,* " Sons of Hashe mthe Gizonite " (I Chron. xi. 34).

JASHOBEAM—son of Zabdiel and one of David's mighty men (I Chron. xi 11).

JASHUB—1. Son of Issachar (Num. xxvi. 24). *Variant,* Job (Gen. xlvi. 13). 2. One of the " sons of Bani " (Ezra x. 29).

JASHUBI - LEHEM—probably the founder of a Judahite family (I Chron. iv. 22).

JASON—Paul's host at Thessalonica (Acts xvii. 6 ff.), and possibly identical with Paul's " kinsman " (Rom. vxi. 21).

JATHNIEL—a son of Meshelemiah (I Chron. xxvi. 2).

JAZIZ—Chief shepherd over David's flocks (1 Chron. xxvii. 31).

JEATERAI—a Gershonite Levite (I Chron. vi. 21). *Variant,* Ethni (ver. 41).

JEBERECHIAH—father of Zechariah (Isaiah viii. 2).

JECHILIAH—mother of King Uzziah (II Chron. xxvi. 3). *Equivalent,* Jecholiah.

JEDAIAH—1. A Simeonite chief (I Chron. lv. 37). 2. One of those who helped to rebuild the wall of Jerusalem (Neh. iii. 10). 3. A returned exile (Zech. vi. 9). 4. A priest (I Chron. ix. 10).

JEDIAEL—1. The founder of a Benjamite clan (I Chron. vii. 6 ff.). 2. One of David's heroes (I Chron. xi. 45). 3. A Korahite porter (I Chron. xxvi. 2).

JEDIDAH—mother of Josiah (II Kings xxi. 1).

JEDIDIAH—name given by Nathan to Solomon (II Sam. xii. 25).

JEDUTHUN—one of the three chief singers or name of a musical guild (1 Chron. ix. 16 and Neh. xi. 17) *Equivalent,* Ethan.

JEHALELEEL — 1. A Calebite (I Chron. iv. 16). 2. A Levite (II Chron. xxix. 12).

JEHDEIAH—1. One of David's overseers (I Chron. xxvii. 30). 2. A Levite (I Chron. xxiv. 20).

JEHEZEKEL—a priest (I Chron. xxiv. 16). *Equivalent,* Ezekiel.

JEHIAH—a Levite (I Chron. xv. 24).

JEHIEL—1. Name of two Levites (I Chron. xv. 18, 20). 2. One of David's courtiers (I Chron. xxvii. 32). 3. A son of Jehoshaphat (II Chron. xxi. 2). 4. A priest (II Chron. 35. 8). 5. A Levite chief (I Chron. xxiii. 8). *Variant,* Jehieli. 6. Father of Obadiah (Ezra viii. 9). 7. One of the " sons of Elam " (Ezra x. 2). 8. A priest of the sons of Harim (Ezra x. 21). 9. A Levite (II Chron. xxix 14).

JEHIELI—*see* Jehiel.

JEHIZKIAH—an Ephraimite chief (II Chron. xxviii 12).

JEHOADAH — *see* Jarah.

JEHOADDAN—mother of Amaziah (II Kings xiv. 2).

JEHOAHAZ—1. Son and successor of Jehu (II Kings x. 35). 2. Third son of Josiah (II Kings xxiii, 30). *Variant,* Shallum. 3. Identical with Ahaziah, king of Judah (II Chron. xxi. 17, *margin*).

JEHOASH—1. Son of Ahaziah and king of Judah (II Kings xi. ff.). 2. Son of Jehoahaz and king of Israel (II Kings xiii. 10. ff.). *Variant*, Joash.

JEHOHANAN—1. A Korahite porter (I Chron. xxvi. 3). 2. One of Jehoshaphat's officers (II Chron. xvii. 15). 3. A priest of Jehoiakim's time (Neh. xii. 13). 4. A priest in the days of Nehemiah (Neh. xii. 42). 5. One of the " sons of Bebai " (Ezra x. 28). 6. Son of Eliashib (Ezra x. 6). *Variant*, Johanan.

JEHOIACHIN—King of Judah, taken captive by Nebuchadnezzar (II Kings xxiv. 8 ff.). *Variants*, Jeconiah, Jechonias, Coniah.

JEHOIADA— 1. Father of Benaiah (II Sam. viii. 18). 2. High priest during reign of Ahaziah and ff. (II Kings xii. 10). 3. One who helped repair the wall of Jerusalem (Neh. iii. 6).

JEHOIAKIM—son of Josiah and King of Judah (II Kings xxiii. 34). *Equivalent*, Eliakim.

JEHOIARIB—name of one of the twenty-four classes of priests (I Chron. ix. 10).

JEHONADAB—1. Nephew of David (II Sam. xiii. 3). 2. Son of Rechab (II. Kings. x. 15 ff.). *Variant*, Ionadab.

JEHONATHAN—*see* Jonathan.

JEHORAM—1. King of Israel after his brother Ahaziah (II Kings iii. 1). 2. Son of Jehoshaphat and King of Judah (II Kings viii. 16). *Variant*, Joram. 3. Son of Toi (II Sam. viii. 10). 4. A Levite (I Chron. xxvi. 25). 5. A priest (II Chron. xvii. 8).

JEHOSHABEATH—wife of Jehoiada (II Chron. xxii. 11). *Variant*, Jehosheba.

JEHOSHAPHAT—1. Son of Asa (I Kings xv. 24). 2. Father of Jehu (II Kings ix. 14). 3. One of Solomon's officers (I Kings iv. 17). 4. Recorder under David (II Sam. viii. 16). 5. One of David's heroes (I Chron. xi. 43). 6. One of David's trumpeters (I Chron. xv. 24). *Equivalents*, Joshaphat, Josaphat.

JEHOSHEBA—*see* Jehoshabeath.

JEHOSHUA—*See* Joshua.

JEHOVAH—the name assigned to God in profound veneration by the Hebrews and frequently used as a component part in compound personal names, as -JIREH (Gen. xxii. 14). -NISSI (Ex. xvii. 15). -SHALOM (Judg. vi. 24). -SHAMAIAH (Ezek. xlviii. 35). -TSIDKENU (Jer. xxiii. 6).

JEHOZABAD—1. One of the conspirators against King Joash (II Kings xii. 21). 2. Second son of Obed-edom (I Chron. xxvi. 4). 3. Officer of Jehoshaphat (II Chron. xvii. 18).

JEHOZADAK—father of the high priest Jeshua

(I Chron. vi. 14 f.). *Variants*, Jozadak, Josedech.

JEHU—1. Son of Hanani (I Kings xvi. 1). 2. Son of Jehoshaphat (II Kings ix. f.). 3. One of David's heroes (I Chron. xii. 3). 4. Son of Obed (I Chron. ii. 38). 5. Son of Josibiah (I Chron. iv. 35).

JEHUBBAH—an Asherite (I Chron. vii. 34).

JEHUCAL—one of Zedekiah's officers (Jer. xxxvii. 3). *Variant*, Jucal.

JEHUDI—an officer of Jehoiakim (Jer. xxvi. 14 ff.).

JEIEL, JEHIEL—1. Head of a Reubenite clan (I Chron. v. 7). 2. Ancestor of Saul (I Chron. ix. 35). 3. One of David's heroes (I Chron. xi. 44). 4, 5. Name of two Levites (I Chron. xv. 18 and II Chron. xxxv. 9). 6. A scribe of Uzziah's (II Chron. xxvi. 11). 7. One of the "sons of Nebo" (Ezra x. 43). *Variant*, Jeuel.

JEKAMEAM—head of a family of Levites (I Chron. xxiii. 19).

JEKAMIAH—1. A descendant of Jerahmeel (I Chron. ii. 41). 2. Son of Jaconiah (I Chron. iii. 18). *Variant*, Jecamiah.

JEKUTHIEL—father of Zanoah (I Chron. iv. 18).

JEMIMAH—Job's eldest daughter (Job. xlii. 14).

JEMUEL—a son of Simeon (Gen. xlvi. 10). *Variant*, Nemuel, *margin*.

JEPHTHAH—" the Gileadite," one of the judges of Israel (Judg. xii. 7). *Variant*, Jephthae.

JEPHUNNEH — 1. Father of Caleb (Num. xiii. 6). 2. Son of Jether (I Chron. vii. 38).

JERAH—son of Joktan (Gen. x. 26) ; otherwise, probably a clan name.

JERAHMEEL — 1. A tribe, or clan, friendly to David during his exile (I Sam. xxvii. 10). 2. Name of a sub-division of Levites (I Chron. xxiv. 29). 3. " Son of Hammeleck " (Jer. xxxvi. 26).

JEREMAI—one of the sons of Hashum (Ezra x. 33).

JEREMIAH — 1. A man of Libnah (II Kings xxiii. 31). 2. A Benjamite bowman (I Chron. xii. 4). 3. Head of a family of Manasseh (I Chron. v. 24). 4. Son of Habazziniah, a Rechabite (Jer. xxxv. 3). 5, 6. Two Gadites, supporters of David (I Chron. xii. 10, 13). 7. A priest who returned with Zerubbabel (Neh. xii. 1). 8. A priest who sealed the covenant (Ezra x. 2). 9. The great prophet, who prophesied during the reign of Josiah and his sons (*see* Book of *Jeremiah*, which is largely autobiographical). *Variants*, Jeremy (Matt. ii. 17) and Jeremias (Matt. xv. 14).

JEREMIAS—*see* Jeremiah, 9.

JEREMOTH—1, 2. Two Benjamites (I Chron. vii. 8., viii. 14). 3. A Levite (I Chron. xxiii. 23). 4. A Naphtalite (I Chron. xxvii. 19). 5, 6, 7. Name of three persons who had married foreign wives (Ezra x. 26, 27). *Variant*, Jerimoth, for Nos. 1 and 4.

JEREMY—*see* Jeremiah, 9.

JERIAH—head of one of the Levitical courses (I Chron. xxiii. 19). *Variant,* Jerijah.

JERIBAI—one of David's heroes (I Chron. xi. 46).

JERIEL—a chief of Issachar clan (I Chron. vii. 2).

JERIJAH—*see* Jeriah.

JERIMOTH—1. A Benjamite (I Chron. vii. 7). 2. One of David's warriors (I Chron. xii. 5). 3. A Son of David (II Chron. xi. 18). 4. A musican (I Chron. xxv. 4) (*see* Jeremoth).

JERIOTH—probably wife or daughter of Caleb (I Chron. ii. 18).

JEROBOAM—name of two kings of Israel : 1. Son of Nebat, first king of the northern kingdom (I Kings xi. 26). 2. Son of Joash, under whose reign Israel reached the zenith of her power (II Kings xiv. 23).

JEROHAM—1. Grandfather of Samuel (1 Sam. i. 1). 2. Head of a Benjamite family (I Chron. viii. 27). 3. A priest (I Chron. ix. 12). 4. Father of Joelah and Zebadiah (I Chron. xii. 7). 5. Father of Azariah (II Chron. xxiii. 1). 6. A Danite chief (I Chron. xxvii. 22).

JERUBBAAL—name given to Gideon (Judges vi. 32). *Equivalent,* Jerubbesheth.

JERUBBESHETH—*see* Jerubbaal.

JERUSHA—mother of King Jotham (II Kings xv. 33). *Variant,* Jerushah.

JESHAIAH—1. Descen-
dant of David (I Chron. iii. 21). 2. Descendant of Moses (I Chron. xxvi. 25). 3. A Merarite Levite (Ezra viii. 19). 4. Descendant of Benjamin (Neh. xi. 7). 5. A Levite musician (I Chron. xxv. 3). 6 A leader under Ezra (Ezra viii. 7).

JESHARELAH—a Levite musician (I Chron. xxv. 14).

JESHEBEAB—a Levite, head of the fourteenth course of priests (I Chron. xxiv. 13).

JESHER—son of Caleb (I. Chron. ii. 18).

JESHISHAI—a Gadite (I Chron. v. 14).

JESHOHAIAH—a Simeonite (I Chron. iv. 36).

JESHUA — 1. A name used for Joshua the son of Nun (Neh. viii. 17). 2. Head of the ninth course of priests (I Chron. xxiv. 11). *Variant,* Jeshuah AV. 3. A Levite (II Chron. xxxi. 15). 4. Name of a family of Pahath-moab (Ezra ii. 6). 5. The high priest who returned with Zerubbabel (Ezra ii. 2). *Variant,* Joshua. 6. A Levitical family who helped rebuild the temple (Ezra iii. 9). 7. A priestly family (Ezra ii. 36).

JESHURUN—an idealistic designation, of honour or affection, for Israel (Deut. xxxii. 15).

JESIMIEL—a Simeonite (I Chron. iv. 36).

JESSE—a Bethlehemite, grandson of Boaz and father of David (I Sam. xvi. 1.ff.).

JESUS—the Greek form of Joshua, or Jeshua: 1. *Re*

Joshua, the son of Nun (Acts vii. 45, *margin*). 2. *Re* Justus, a co-worker with Paul (Col. iv. 11). 3. *Re* Jose, an ancestor of our Lord (RV. Luke iii.29).

JESUS CHRIST—the supreme personality of Scripture around Whom everything else centres. The Old Testament leads up to Him as the central figure in the Divine Revelation and on every page of the New Testament we see the impress of His life. He was the Son of the Virgin Mary, and was born in the caravanserai at Bethlehem of Judah. Prophets foretold His coming and miracles hailed His birth. Humble shepherds united with learned magi about the manger in which He was born. His boyhood and early manhood were spent in Nazareth of Galilee in comparative obscurity, save for one visit to the temple at Jerusalem at twelve years of age in order to become a " son of the Law." He was manifested to the Jews by the baptism of John, after which He passed through a period of temptation in the wilderness. During His earthly ministry He "went about doing good." His miracles were all beneficial. Nearly all classes foregathered with Him, though the ruling classes misunderstood Him and resented His words to them. Their suspicion and ill-will ultimately led to His crucifixion under Pontius Pilate.

He subsequently rose from the dead, and in His resurrection is the promise of our own. The Gospels furnish the fullest account of His life and teaching that we have, though Josephus makes a brief allusion to Him. The Gospels thus furnish the best text-books for the study of His life, whilst we can note the development and effect of His teaching in the *Epistles* and in the *Acts of the Apostles.*

JETHER—1. Father-in-law of Moses (Ex. iv. 18)— a probable error for Jethro. 2. Firstborn son of Gideon (Judg. viii. 20). 3. Ishmaelite husband of Abigail (I Chron. ii. 17). 4. A man of Asher (I Chron. vii. 38). 5, 6. Two men of Judah (I Chron. ii. 32 ; iv. 17).

JETHETH—an Edomite clan-chief (Gen. xxxvi. 40).

JETHRO—an Arab sheik and priest of the Kenites, the father-in-law of Moses (Ex. iv. 18). *Equivalents* (probably) Jether, Reuel, Hobab.

JEUEL—1. A Judahite clan-chief (I Chron. ix. 6). 2. A Levite (II Chron. xxix. 13). 3. A leader under Ezra (Ezra viii. 13). *Variant*, for Nos. 2 and 3, Jeiel (AV).

JEUSH—1. A son of Esau (Gen. xxxvi. 5). 2. A Benjamite chief (I. Chron. vii. 10). 3. A Levitical family (I Chron. xxiii. 10 f.). 4. A descendant of Saul (I Chron. viii. 39). 5. Son of Rehoboam (II

Chron. xi. 19). *Variant*, Jehush.

JEUZ—a Benjamite (I Chron. viii. 10).

JEZANIAH—*see* Jaazaniah.

JEZEBEL—daughter of Ethbaal, king of Tyre; wife of King Ahab. As a zealous Baal-worshipper, she exercised an evil influence in the land of Israel, and came into conflict with Elijah (I Kings xviii. 19). In Apocalyptic literature her name is the symbol of wickedness and idolatry (Rev. ii. 20).

JEZER—head of the Jezerites (Num. xxvi. 49).

JEZIEL—a soldier of David (I Chron. xii. 3).

JEZRAHIAH—a singer, associated with Ezra the priest (Neh. xii. 42). *Variant*, Izrahiah.

JIDLAPH—son of Nahor (Gen. xxii. 22).

JOAB — 1. Son of Zeruiah, David's sister (II Sam. xx. 23). 2. A Judahite, descendant of Caleb (I Chron. ii. 54). 3. A family of exiles with Zerubbabel (Ezra ii. 6). 4. The son of Seraiah (I Chron. iv. 14).

JOAH — 1. An officer under Hezekiah (II Kings xviii. 18). 2. An officer under Josiah (II Chron. xxxiv. 8). 3. A Levite porter (I Chron. xxvi. 4). 4. A Levitical family name—identical with Ethan—(I Chron. vi. 21 ; v. 42).

JOAHAZ—father of Joah (II Chron. xxxiv. 8).

JOANNA — 1. Ancestor of Jesus (Luke iii. 27). 2. Wife of Chuza, steward of Herod Antipas ; as a devoted disciple of Jesus, she ministered to his needs and, after the crucifixion, helped to embalm His body (Luke viii. 3).

JOASH—1. Father of Gideon (Judges vi. 11). 2. A son of King Ahab (I Kings xxii. 26). 3. A descendant of Judah (I Chron. iv. 22). 4. A Benjamite (I Chron. xii. 3). 5. A son of Belchar (I Chron. vii. 8). 6. A servant of David (I Chron. xxvii. 28).

JOB—the patriarch, conspicuous as an example of patient endurance of undeserved suffering who, together with his friends Eliphaz, Bildad, Zophar and also Elihu, in their famous colloquies, " strive to justify the ways of God with men " (*see* Book of *Job* and cf. Ezek. xiv. 12-20, and James v. 11).

Note—The question of authenticity, the identity of the Satan the " tempter " or adversary of Job, etc., is one for modern criticism : the present reference is concerned merely with the popular aspect of the story.

JOBAB — 1. Son of Joktan (Gen. x. 29). 2. The second king of Edom (Gen. xxxvi. 33 f.). 3. A king of Madon (Josh. xi. 1). 4, 5. Name of two Benjamites (I Chron. viii. 9, 18).

JOCHEBED—wife of Amram and mother of Aaron and Moses (Ex. vi. 20).

JOED—a Benjamite (Neh. xi. 7).

JOEL— 1. One of the minor prophets (*see* Book of *Joel*).

2. Son of Samuel (I Sam. viii. 2). 3. Ancestor of Samuel (I Chron. vi. 36). *Variant,* Shaul. 4. A Reubenite (I Chron. v. 4). 5, 6, 7. Levites (I Chron. xv. 7, xxiii. 8, II Chron. xxix. 12). 8. A Gadite (I Chron. v. 12). 9. A Simeonite prince (I Chron. iv. 35). 10. One of David's heroes (I Chron. xi. 38). 11. A Manassite chief (I Chron. xxvii. 20). 12. One who married a foreign wife (Ezra x. 43). 13. A Benjamite overseer (Neh. xi. 9).

JOELAH—one of David's warriors (I Chron. xii. 7).

JOEZER—one of David's soldiers (I Chron. xii. 6).

JOGLI—a Danite (Num. xxxiv. 22).

JOHA — 1. One of David's heroes (I Chron. xi. 45). 2. A Benjamite (I Chron. viii. 16).

JOHANAN—1. One of Zedakiah's captains (II Kings xxv. 23). 2. Eldest son of King Josiah (I Chron. iii. 15). 3. A descendant of David (I Chron. iii. 24). 4. A leader under Ezra (Ezra viii. 12). 5, 6. Two soldiers who joined David (I. Chron. xii. 4, 12). 7. An Ephraimite (II Chron. xxviii. 12). 8. A high priest (I Chron. vi. 9 ff.). (*see* Jehohanan).

JOHN—1. The father of Simon Peter (Matt. xvi. 17). *Variants,* Bar-Jona, Jonas. 2. Member of the Sanhedrin (Acts iv. 6). 3. The Apostle and Evangelist, son of Zebedee and brother of James (Mark i.

19). 4. The Baptist, forerunner of the Lord (Luke chap. i.).

JOHN MARK—co-missionary with Barnabas (his uncle) and Paul (Acts xii. 25) (*see* Mark.)

JOIADA—a high priest, son of Eliashab (Neh. xii. 10 f.).

JOIAKIM—a high priest, son of Jeshua (Neh. xii. 10 ff.).

JOIARIB—1. A descendant of Perez (Neh. xi. 5). 2. Head of a priestly family (Neh. xi. 10). *Variant,* Jehoiarib (I Chron. ix. 10). 3. A teacher under Ezra (Ezra viii. 16).

JOKIM—name of a post-exilic family (I Chron. iv. 22).

JOKSHAN—son of Abraham (Gen. xxv. 2). Probably identical with Joktan.

JOKTAN—one of the two sons of Eber (Gen. x. 25 ff.).

JONA and JONAS—*see* John.

JONAH—the son of Amittai ; the prophet of Israel whom the Lord commissioned to preach against Nineveh and announce impending doom. Objections to the identity of the prophet and to the historicity of the book he wrote have left modern scholars divided— everything impinges on the question of interpretation, whether allegorical, symbolical, mythological, or historical. Probably the " fish " incident has been over-stressed, so that the main purpose of the book, viz., to arraign and rebuke the narrow, intolerant religiosity of the Jews and to teach that Jehovah is the God of the Gentile as well as of the Jew, has been largely obscured. The value of the book is in nowise lessened by the fact that parallels to Jonah are found in Greek, Babylonian and Buddhist mythologies (cf. II Kings xiv. 25 and Jonah i. ff.).

JONAN—an ancestor of Jesus (Luke iii. 30).

JONAS—*see* John.

JONATHAN—1. A son of King Saul; a brave and attractive personality, whose loyal and beautiful friendship with David has captivated the heart of the world (I Sam. xiv. 6, 8). 2. Son of Gershom and a descendant of Moses (Judges xviii. 30). 3. A son of Abiathar a high priest (II Sam. xv. 27). 4. A son of Shimeah (II Sam. xxi. 21). 5. A son of Uzziah, one of David's treasurers (I Chron. xxvii. 25). 6. One of David's heroes (II Sam. xxiii. 32). 7. A priestly son of Joiada (Neh. xii. 11). *Variant,* Johanan. 8. A son of Jada (I. Chron. ii. 32). 9. Father of Ebed (Ezra viii. 6). 10. A priest (Neh. xii. 14). 11. A scribe in whose house Jeremiah was imprisoned (Jer. xxxvii. 15). 12. A son of Shemaiah (Neh. xii. 18). 13. A son of Kareah (Jer. xl. 8).

JORAH—head of a postexilic Jewish family (Ezra ii. 18). *Variant,* Hariph.

JORAI—head of a Gadite family (I Chron. v. 13).

JORAM — 1. A Levite (I Chron. xxvi. 25). 2. Son of Toi (II Sam. viii. 10). 3, 4. Two kings so named (*see* Jehoram.)

JORIM—ancestor of Jesus (Luke iii. 29).

JORKOAM—a Judahite family (I Chron. ii. 44).

JOSEDEK—*see* Jehozadak.

JOSEPH—1. Eldest son of Jacob and Rachel. His career is packed with dramatic incidents : sold by his brothers into captivity ; his purchase by Potiphar ; his rise at Pharaoh's court; his rescue of his brethren from famine, leading to family reconciliation. These stamp his as one of the most romantic stories of any literature and warrant his being regarded as the type of an ideal faith which, amid all fluctuating circumstances, recognizes a Divine destiny (Gen. xxx. 24 and chaps. xxxvii-l.). 2. A man of Issachar (Num. xiii. 7). 3. A son of Asaph (I Chron. xxv. 2). 4. A son of Bani (Ezra x. 42). 5. A priest (Neh. xii. 14). 6, 7. Two of our Lord's ancestors (Luke iii. 24, 30). 8. The husband of Mary and " father " of Jesus (Matt. i. 20). 9. J. of Arimathea (Mark xv. 43).

JOSEPH-BARSABAS—a candidate with Matthias as successor to Judas in the Apostolate (Acts i. 23) (*see* Barsabas.)

JOSES — 1. One of our Lord's brothers (Matt. xiii. 55). 2. Barnabas' natal name (Acts iv. 36).

JOSHAH—a Simeonite chief (I Chron. iv. 34).

JOSHAPHAT — 1. One of David's heroes (I Chron. xi. 43). 2. A priest (I Chron. xv. 24).

JOSHAVIAH—one of David's heroes (I Chron. xi. 46).

JOSHBEKASHAH—a son of Heman (I Chron. xxv. 4), if it be read as a proper name.

JOSHUA—1. Son of Nun; successor of Moses (Deut. xxxi. 7, 14, 23; Num. xiii. 8, 16 and Book of J). Variant Jehoshua. Equivalents, Oshea, Hoshea. 2. A man of Bethshemesh (I Sam. vi. 14, 18). 3. A governor of Jerusalem (II Kings xxiii. 8). 4. The son of Jehozadak (Ezra ii. 2). Greeek form, Jesus (which see).

JOSIAH — 1. King of Judah (II Kings xxii. 1). 2. Son of Zephaniah (Zech. vi. 10).

JOSIBIAH—a Simeonite chief (I Chron. iv. 35).

JOSIPHIAH—The father of Shelomith (Ezra viii. 10).

JOTHAM—1. Son of Jerubbaal (Judg. ix. 5). 2. Son of Uzziah and king of Judah (II Kings xv. 5). 3. A son of Jehdai (I Chron. ii. 47). Variant, Joatham.

JOZABAD—1, 2, 3. Name of three of David's soldiers (I Chron. xii. 4). 4, 5, 6, 7, 8, 9. Name of six Levites (II Chron. xxxi. 13, xxxv. 9; Ezra viii. 33, x. 23; Neh. viii. 7, xi. 16). 10. A priest (Ezra x. 22).

JOZACHAR—one of the murderers of King Joash (II Kings xii. 21). Equivalent, Zabad (II Chron. xxiv. 26).

JOZADAK—see Jehozadak.

JUBAL—son of Lamech and fabled inventor of the art of music (Gen. iv. 21) (see Jabal).

JUCAL—an opposer of Jeremiah (Jer. xxxviii. 1).

JUDA—ancestor of Jesus (Luke iii. 26).

JUDAH—1. A Levite (Ezra iii. 9). 2. An overseer (Neh. xi. 9). 3. Son of a priest (Neh. xii. 36).

JUDAS—1. One of our Lord's brothers (Mark vi. 3). 2. J. Barsabas, see Barsabas. 3. J. of Damascus—in whose abode Paul lodged (Acts ix. 11). 4. J. of Galilee—an agitator against Roman taxation levied by Quirinius (Acts v. 37).

JUDAS ISCARIOT—one of the twelve disciples, the betrayer of Jesus; his remorse and tragic fate show him to have been largely the tool of Satan (Mark iii. 19).

JUDE—" a servant of Jesus Christ, and brother of James " (see Epistle of Jude).

JUDITH—1. Daughter of Beeri, wife of Esau (Gen. xxvi. 34).

JULIA—one of a group of persons greeted by Paul (Rom. xvi. 15).

JULIUS—a centurion, custodian of Paul on journey to Rome (Acts xxvii. 1).

JUNIA—one of a group of persons greeted by Paul (Rom. xvi. 7).

JUSHAB-HESED—son of Zerubbabel (I Chron. iii. 20).

JUSTUS—surname given to three people in N. T. 1. Joseph Barsabas (Acts i. 23 ff.). 2. Titus, Paul's host in Corinth (Acts xviii. 7 f.). 3. A Jew named Jesus (Cols. iv. 11).

K

KADMIEL—a Levite who returned with Zerubbabel (Ezra ii. 40).

KALLAI—a priest of the family of Sallai (Neh. xii 20).

KEDAR—second son of Ishmael (Gen. xxv. 13).

KEDEMAH—youngest son of Ishmael (Gen. xxv. 15).

KELITA—a Levite with Ezra (Neh. viii. 7).

KEMUEL—1. Father of Aram (Gen. xxii. 21). 2. Son of Shiphtan (Num. xxxiv. 24). 3. Father of Hashabiah in David's time (I Chron. xxvii. 17).

K E N A Z—1. A son of Eliphaz (Gen. xxxvi. 11). 2. Grandson of Othniel (Josh. xv. 17).

KEREN-HAPPUCH—the youngest of Job's three daughters (Job. xlii. 14).

KEZIA—the second of Job's daughters (Job. xlii. 14).

K I S H—1. A Benjamite ; son of Jehiel (I Chron. viii. 30). 2. Father of King Saul (I Sam. ix. 1). 3. A Levite in David's time (I Chron. xxiii. 21). 4. Ancestor of Mordecai (Esther ii. 5).

KOHATH—second son of Levi, and founder of the great Kohathite family (Gen. xlvi. 11).

KOLAIAH—father of a certain prophet Ahab put to death by Nebuchadrezzar (Jer. xxix. 21).

KORAH—1. Grandson of Esau (Gen. xxxvi. 16). 2. Sor of Izhar ; the leader of a rebellion against Moses and Aaron (see Num. xvi. 1 to xvii. 13.)

KORE—1. A descendant of the first Korah (I Chron. xxvi. 1). 2. A Levite, son of Imnah (II Chron. xxxi. 14).

KUSHAIAH—a Levite, father of Ethan (I Chron. xv. 17).

L

LAADAH—son of Shelah (I Chron. iv. 21).

LAADAN—1. An Ephraimite in the ancestry of Joshua (I Chron. vii. 26). 2. A Gershonite in the time of David (I Chron. xxiii. 7).

LABAN—a son of Bethuel. Brother of Rebekah. When Jacob fled from Esau's vengeance it was to Laban he went. He served Laban seven years for Rachel, but had Leah handed to him by a trick. He served seven years more for Rachel and six for the cattle he took, leaving Laban at the end of twenty years. (Gen. xxiv. 1-67.)

LAEL—a Gershonite, father of Elisaph (Num. iii. 24).

LAHAD—a son of Jahath, a man of Judah (I Chron. iv. 2).

LAHMI—the brother of Go-

liath the Gittite, and, like him, a giant. He was slain by Elhanan (I Chron. xx. 5).

LAISH—a man of Gallim (I Sam. xxv. 44).

LAMECH—1. A son of Methusael of the race of Cain. He boasts of having slain a young man, and seems to have feared a sevenfold vengeance (Gen. iv. 18-24). 2. An antediluvian patriarch of the race of Seth (Gen. v. 25).

LAPPIDOTH—husband of Deborah the prophetess (Judg. iv. 4).

LAZARUS—1. The name given to the beggar in the parable of "The Rich Man and Lazarus" (Luke xvi 19-31). 2. A member of the Bethany family; brother of Mary and Martha. He was miraculously raised from the dead by Christ. Strangely enough, no spoken word of his has been recorded (John xi. 1.)

LEAH—eldest daughter of Laban; married Jacob (Gen. xxix. 16-35).

LEMUEL—the king to whom is ascribed *Proverbs* chapter xxxi. (which *see*).

LEVI—Jacob's third son (Gen. xxix. 34). Three others of this name are mentioned; *see* Luke iii. 29; Luke iii 24. Here we note that Levi was another name of Matthew (Mark ii. 14).

LIBNI—elder son of Gershon (Ex. vi. 17).

LIKHI—a Manassite, a son of Shemidah (I Chron. vii. 19).

LINUS—a Christian at Rome who joined Paul in salutations to Timothy (II Timothy iv. 21).

LOIS—grandmother of Timothy; a woman of "unfeigned faith" (II Tim. i. 5).

LOTAN—a duke, a son of Seir (Gen. xxxvi. 20).

LUCIUS—1. A Christian from Cyrene (Acts xiii. 1). 2. A Christian with Paul at Corinth (Rom. xvi. 21).

LUD—fourth son of Shem (Gen. x. 22).

LUKE (also called LUCAS) " the beloved physician." He was a companion of Paul, accompanying him on several parts of his missionary journeys. His help was doubtless valuable from a medical point of view, but he seems to have been a thoroughly helpful companion in other ways also. He is the author of the Gospel which bears his name and most probably of the Book of the *Acts* also (Col. iv. 14).

LYDIA—a woman of Thyatira, who made a living at Philippi by purple dyeing. She welcomed Paul and Silas on their arrival there. She appears to have been a sincere believer and a generous helper in the Christian Church at Philippi (Acts xvi. 14).

LYSANIAS—a tetrarch of Abilene (Luke iii. 1).

M

MAACHAH—Nine people of this name are mentioned in Scripture, none of who is of outstanding importance. The following are the references : Gen. xxii. 24 ; I Chron. vii. 15 ; I Chron. ii. 48 ; I Chron. viii. 29 ; II Sam. iii. 3 ; I Chron. xi. 43 ; I Chron. xxvii. 16 ; I Kings ii. 39 ; I Kings xv. 2.

MAADAI—a son of Bani (Ezra x. 34).

MAADIAH—a priest who returned from exile in Babylon (Neh. xii. 5).

MAAI—a priest's son (Neh. xii. 36).

MAASEIAH—nineteen persons of this name are mentioned in Scripture. The following are the references : I Chron. xv. 18 ; II Chron. xxiii. 1 ; II Chron. xxvi. 11 ; II Chron. xxviii. 7 ; II Chron. xxiv. 8 ; Jer. li. 59 ; Jer. xxix. 21 ; Jer. xxix. 25 ; Jer. xxxv. 4 ; Neh. xi. 5 ; Neh. xi. 7 ; Ezra x. 18 ; Ezra x. 21 ; Ezra x. 22 ; Ezra x. 30 ; Neh. iii. 23 ; Nch. x. 25 ; Neh. xi. 41 (two priests).

MAASIAI—a priest; son of Adiel (I Chron. ix. 12).

MAATH—father of Nagge (Luke iii. 26).

MAAZ—grandson of Jerameel (I Chron. ii 27).

MAAZIAH—head of the twenty-fourth course of the priesthood (I Chron. xxiv. 18).

MACHBANAI—the eleventh of the Gadite heroes who joined David at Ziklag (I Chron. xii. 13).

MACHI—the representative spy from Gad (Num. xiii. 15).

MACHIR—1. Eldest son of Manasseh (Josh. xvii. 1). 2. Son of Ammiel. He brought provisions to David during the Absalom rebellion (II Sam. ix. 4).

MACHNADEBAI—a son of Bani in Ezra's time (Ezra x. 40).

MADAI—third son of Japheth (Gen. x. 2).

MAGDIEL—a duke descended from Esau. (Gen. xxxvi. 43.)

MAGOG—second son of Japheth (Gen. x. 2).

MAHALALEEL—1. The son of Cainan (Gen. v. 12-17). 2. Son of Perez (Neh. xi. 4).

MAHALI—eldest son of Merari (Ex. vi. 19).

MAHARAI—one of David's mighty men (II Sam. xxiii. 28).

MAHATH—a Levite in Hezekiah's time (II Chron. xxxi. 13).

MAHAZIOTH—a Levite—descendant of Heman (I Chron. xxv. 4).

MAHER - SHALAL - HASH-BAZ—the name (meaning " speed, Spoil ; hurry, Prey ") given to one of Isaiah's sons (Isaiah viii. 1).

MAHLAH—eldest daughter of Zelophehad (Num. xxvi. 33).

MAHLON—elder son of Elimelech and Naomi ; married Orpah, but died early (Ruth i. 2-5).

MAHOL—father of Heman (I Kings iv. 31).

MALACHI—the name of the last of the Minor Prophets, though as the word simply means " My messenger," the book may be regarded as anonymous.

MALCHAM — 1. A Benjamite, son of Shaharaim (I Chron. viii. 9). 2. Another name for Milcom (Ammonite deity) (which see).

MALCHIAH—a son of Zedekiah (Jer. xxxviii. 6).

MALCHIEL—a son of Beriah (Gen. xlvi. 17).

MALCHIJAH—there are eleven persons of this name, though there is some variety in the spelling of it. References are as follows : I Chron. vi. 40 ; I Chron. xxiv. 9 ; I Chron. ix. 12 ; two sons of Parosh, Ezra x. 25 ; Neh. iii. 11 ; Neh. iii. 31 ; Neh. viii. 4 ; Neh. x. 3 ; Neh. xii. 42.

MALCHIRAM—a son of king Jechoniah (I Chron. iii. 18).

MALCHI-SHUA—a son of King Saul (I Sam. xiv. 49).

MALCHUS—the high priest's servant whose ear Peter cut off (John xviii. 10).

MALLOTHI—a son of Heman (I Chron. xxv. 4).

MALLUCH—six unimportant people bear this name. The references are as follows : I Chron. vi. 44 ; Neh. xii. 2 ; Ezra x. 29 ; Ezra x. 32 ; Neh. x. 4 ; Neh. x. 27.

MANAEN—a Christian prophet or teacher in the Church at Antioch (Acts xiii. 1).

MANAHATH—son of Shobal (Gen. xxxvi. 23).

MANASSEH — 1. Elder son of Joseph (Gen. xli. 51). 2. Father of a certain Gershom (Judg. xviii. 30). 3. Son and successor of Hezekiah (II Chron. xxxiii.

1). 4. Son of Hashum (Ezra x. 33).

MANASSES—king of Judah (Greek form of Manasseh) (Matt. i. 10).

MANOAH—a Danite of Zorah, father of Samson (Judg. xiii. 2).

MAOCH—father of Achish king of Gath (I Sam. xxvii. 2).

MARA—the name Naomi asked to be called (Ruth i. 20).

MARESHAH—father of Hebron (I Chron. ii. 42).

MARK (or MARCUS)—the Evangelist who wrote (under the guidance of Peter) our second Gospel, though the earliest. His full name was John Mark. His mother, Mary, was in good circumstances and held a high position in the early Church. Mark started with Paul and Barnabas on the first missionary journey, but for some reason turned back. This led to Paul refusing to take him on the second journey, so Barnabas, his uncle, took him as his companion. Paul and Mark were reconciled in later life, and in his last imprisonment Paul wrote kindly of him (Acts xii. 25) (see John Mark.)

MARSENA—one of the seven princes of Persia mentioned in Esther i. 14.

MARTHA—apparently the oldest member of the Bethany family (Lazarus and Mary were the other two) ; was " cumbered about much serving," yet was loyal to Christ in a very real way (John xi. 5).

MARY—1. sister of Martha above; seems to have possessed a quiet, devotional character (Luke x. 38-42). 2. Mary, the wife of Clopas or Cleopas, who is apparently identical with Alphæus (Mark xv. 40). 3. Mary the Virgin, the mother of Jesus. The main events of her life are too well known to need recapitulation here (*see* Luke i. 26-56 and the many corresponding references.) 4. Mary of Magdala or Mary Magdalene, out of whom Christ cast seven devils. She was the most prominent of the Marys, other than the Virgin Mary, and seems to have followed Christ with a passionate devotion. She was early at the tomb on the morning of the Resurrection (Mark xvi. 9). 5. Mary the mother of Mark—a woman held in high esteem in the early Church (Acts xii. 12).

MASH — youngest son of Aram (Gen. x. 23).

MASSA—a son of Ishmael (Gen. xxv. 14).

MATRED—the mother of Mehetabel (Gen. xxxvi. 39).

MATTAN—1. A priest of Baal slain before the altar (II Kings xi. 18). 2. Father of Shephatiah in Jeremiah's time (Jer. xxxviii. 1).

MATTANIAH—there are nine men of this name mentioned in Scripture. All are of minor importance. The references are: I Chron. xxv. 4 ; II Chron. xx. 14 ; II Chron. xxix. 13; II Kings xxiv. 17 ; I Chron. ix. 15 ; Ezra x. 26 ; Ezra x. 27 ; Ezra x. 30 ; Ezra x. 37.

MATTATHA—son of Nathan and grandson of King David (Luke iii. 31).

MATTATHAH—son of Hashum (Ezra x. 33).

MATTATHIAS — 1. Son of Semei (Luke iii. 26). 2. Son of a certain Amos (Luke iii. 25).

MATTENAI—1. A priest (Neh. xii. 19). 2. A son of Hashum (Ezra x. 33). 3. A son of Bani (Ezra x. 37).

MATTHAN—a son of Eleazar, and the father of Jacob whose son was Joseph the father of Jesus (Matt. i. 15).

MATTHAT—son of Levi; the father of Jorim (Luke iii. 29).

MATTHEW—a tax-gatherer, who became one of Christ's disciples. The author of the first Gospel. Christ found him at the receipt of customs and called him to discipleship (Matthew ix. 9-13).

MATTHIAS—chosen by the early Church as a disciple to fill Judas' place. Nothing more is known of him (Acts i. 21-26). The other candidate was Barsabas (which *see*).

MATTITHIAH—1. A Levite appointed by David as porter (I Chron. xv. 18). 2. A Korahite Levite, eldest son of Shallum (I Chron. ix. 31). 3. A son of Nebo (Ezra x. 43). 3. A priest or Levite who supported Ezra (Neh. viii. 4).

MEDAD—a man who with

Eldad prophesied in the camp of Israel (Num. xi. 26-29).

MEDAN—a son of Abraham by Keturah (Gen. xxv. 2).

MEHETABEL—1. A daughter of Matred, and wife of Hadar king of Edom (Gen. xxxvi. 39). 2. Father of Delaiah in Nehemiah's time. *Variant*, Mehetabeel (Neh. vi. 10).

MEHIR—a man of Judah (I Chron. iv. 11).

MEHUJAEL—son of Irad (Gen. iv. 18).

MEHUMAN—one of King Ahasuerus' seven chamberlains (Esther i. 10).

MELATIAH—a Gibeonite who helped to build the wall of Jerusalem (Neh. iii. 7).

MELCHI—a name figuring in the ancestry of Jesus (Luke iii. 28 and iii. 24).

MELCHIZEDEK—a mysterious " priest of the most high God," to whom Abraham gave tithes on his return from the victory over the four confederate kings. He is treated in the New Testament as a type of the eternal priesthood (Gen. xiv. 18).

MELEA—Father of Eliakim (Luke iii. 31).

MELECH—a son of Micah (I Chron. viii. 35).

MELICU—a priest in Nehemiah's time (Neh. xii. 14).

MELZAR—the steward set over Daniel; but as the name simply means " the steward," perhaps it may not have been a personal name (Dan. i. 11).

MEMUCAN—one of Ahasue-rus' seven princes (Esther i. 14).

MENAHEM—a son of Gadi; he slew the murderer of King Zechariah and assumed the rule of the northern kingdom. Became a kind of vassal under Pul, king of Assyria. (II Kings xv. 14, etc.)

MEPHIBOSHETH—1. A son of Saul, executed by the Gibeonites (II Sam. xxi. 7). 2. A son of Jonathan who was crippled in childhood through being accidentally dropped by his nurse. Later in life he received great kindness at the hands of David in memory of his father Jonathan (II Sam. iv. 4).

MERAB—Saul's eldest daughter (I Sam. xiv. 49).

MERAIAH—a priest in the days of Joiakim (Neh. xii. 12).

MERAIOTH—1. A priest, the son of Zerahiah (I Chron. vi. 6). 2. A priest in the days of Joiakim (Neh. xii. 15).

MERARI—youngest son of Levi (Gen. xlvi. 11).

MERED—a man of Judah (I Chron. iv. 17).

MEREMOTH—the son of the priest Uriah (Ezra viii. 33)

MERIB-BAAL—a son of Jonathan (I Chron. viii. 34).

MESAHAB—wife of the Edomite king, Hadar (Gen. xxxvi. 39).

MESHA — 1. The firstborn son of Caleb (I Chron. ii. 42). 2. A king of Moab, feudatory of King Ahab, to whom he had to hand over an enormous tribute o lambs (II Kings iii. 4).

MESHACH—the Babylonian name given to Mishael, one of Daniel's companions (Dan. i. 7).

MESHELEMIAH—a son of the Levite Kore (I Chron. ix. 21).

MESHEZABEEL—there are three persons so named. See the following references: Neh. iii. 4; Neh. x 21; Neh. xi. 24.

MESHILLEMOTH — 1. An Ephraimite, father of Berechiah (II Chron. xxviii. 12). 2. Son of Immer (Neh. xi. 13).

MESHULLAM — there are twenty-one men of this name in Scripture, none of whom is of great importance. *See* the following references: I Chron. viii. 19; I Chron. v. 13; II Kings xxii. 3; I Chron. ix. 11; II Chron. xxx iv. 12 I Chron. ix. 12; I Chron. iii. 19; I Chron. ix. 7; I Chron. ix. 8; Ezra viii. 16; Ezra x. 15; Ezra x. 29; Neh. iii. 4; Neh. iii. 6; Neh. viii. 4; Neh. x. 7; Neh. x. 20; Neh. xii. 13; Neh. xii. 16; Neh. xii. 25. Neh. xi. 33.

MESHULLEMETH—daughter of Haruz (II Kings xxi, 19).

MESSIAH—the prophetic name for Jesus. It is the Old Testament *equivalent* for Christ. Both words mean smeared, and therefore signify "anointing;" *the Messiah,* or *the Christ,* means the Anointed One. (Dan. ix. 25, and very many other passages.)

METHUSAEL—the son of Mehujael, and father of Lamech (Gen. iv. 18).

METHUSELAH—son of Enoch and father of Lamech. Is notable as being the longest-lived of any of the dwellers of antiquity, his age being given as 969 years (Gen. v. 21-27).

MIBHAR—one of David's mighty men (I Chron. xi. 38).

MIBSAM—a son of Ishmael (Gen. xxv. 13).

MIBZAR—a duke of Edom (Gen. xxxvi. 42).

MICAH — 1. Moses' uncle. 2. An Ephraimite, whose strange story is told in *Judg.* xvii and xviii. 3. Grandson of Jonathan (I Chron. viii. 34). 4. Micah the Morasthite, the sixth of the Minor Prophets (*see* the book which bears his name). He was a younger contemporary of Isaiah and Hosea. 5. A son of Joel (I Chron. v. 5). 6. The father of Abdon (II Chron. xxxiv. 20). 7. Grandson of Asaph (I Chron. ix. 15).

MICAHIAH (also spelt MICAIAH)—1. Daughter of Uriah (II Chron. xiii. 2). 2. A prophet, the son of Imlah in the days of Ahab (I Kings xxii. 8-28). The other five persons bearing this name are of minor importance. The references are: II Chron. xvii. 7; II Kings xxii. 12; Jer. xxxvi. 11; Neh. xii. 35; Neh. xii. 41.

MICHA—1. A son of Mephibosheth (II Sam. ix. 12). 2. A Levite who sealed the covenant (Neh. x. 11). 3.

Son of Zabdi, and grandson of Asaph (Neh. xi. 17).

MICHAEL — 1. Father of Sethur (Num. xiii. 13). 2. Son of Jeshishai (I Chron. v. 14). 3. A chief man of the tribe of Issachar (I Chron. vii. 3). Others of the same name are referred to in I Chron. v. 13; I Chron. vi. 40; I Chron. viii. 16; I Chron. xii. 20 I Chron. xxvii. 18; II Chron. xxi. 2; Ezra viii. 8. The name is also applied to the archangel in Dan. x. 13, etc.

MICHAL—the younger daughter of King Saul and wife of David (I Sam. xviii. 20).

MICHRI—a Benjamite; father of Uzzi (I Chron. ix. 8).

MIDIAN—the fourth of the sons of Abraham and Keturah (Gen. xxv. 2).

MIJAMIN — a priest; the son of Parosh (Neh. x. 7).

MIKLOTH—a military captain in David's reign (I Chron. xxvii. 4).

MIKNEIAH—a Levite porter who played the harp in David's reign (I Chron. xv. 18).

MILALAI—a priest's son (Neh. xii. 36).

MILCAH—daughter of Haran and sister of Lot (Gen. xi. 29).

MILCOM—the god of the Ammonites identical with Molech (I Kings xi. 33; Zeph. 1. 5). *Equivalent,* Malcham—(which *see*).

MINIAMIN—a Levite of the temple during Hezekiah's reign (II Chron. xxxi. 15).

MIRIAM—the sister of Aaron. She watched over the ark wherein was the infant Moses, and, on the bidding of the Egyptian princess, summoned her mother as nurse to the child. A famous song of Miriam has been preserved (Ex. ii. 4-8).

MIRMA—a Benjamite, son of Shararaim (I Chron. viii. 10).

MISHAEL — 1. A son of Uzziel (Ex. vi. 22). 2. One of Daniel's three companions (Dan. i. 6). 3. A supporter of Ezra (Neh. viii. 4).

MISHAM—a son of Elpaal (I Chron. viii. 12).

MISHMA—fifth son of Ishmael (Gen. xxv. 14).

MITHREDATH—1. The treasurer under Cyrus (Ezra i. 8). 2. One of those who complained to Artaxerxes (Ezra iv. 7).

MIZRAIM—second son of Ham (Gen. x. 6).

MIZZAH—a son of Reuel (Gen. xxxvi. 13).

MNASON—a Christian from Cyprus; one of the early disciples (Acts xxi. 16). ·

MOAB—son of Lot (incestuous) (Gen. xix. 37).

MORDECAI—a Benjamite, guardian of Esther, in the story of whom he figures prominently. He had saved the king's life at one time, and this incident proved to be a source of deliverance for the Jews from Haman's plot (Esther ii. 5-20).

MOSES—one of the outstanding men in world history. Born during the Israelitish bondage in

Egypt and of Jewish parents, he was, through the divinely guided strategy of his mother, taken into Pharaoh's palace under the care of an Egyptian princess. His mother, who acted as his nurse, appears to have nurtured him in the great traditions of his race. He rendered good service to Pharaoh, according to Josephus. In early manhood, being moved by an act of cruelty to one of his race, he slew an Egyptian. He was led to take refuge in the wilderness for a time. At length, when his character had matured, he was called to lead his race out of bondage along the path of racial freedom and development. He was assisted by his brother Aaron. For many years under God's guidance he shaped the destinies of his people. He was their great lawgiver, and led them to the borders of the promised land. He died after having a view of the land he might not enter as leader and was buried in a valley in Moab. He was present, according to the Gospel story, at the transfiguration of Christ (*see* the whole Book of *Exodus*, etc., for references to his life).

MOZA—1. A son of Caleb (I Chron. ii. 46). 2. A descendant of Jonathan (I Chron. viii. 36).

MUPPIM—the eighth son of Benjamin (Gen. xlvi. 21).

MUSHI—younger son of Merari (Ex. vi. 19).

N

NAAM—a son of Caleb (I Chron. iv. 15).

NAAMAH—1. Daughter of Lamech (Gen. iv. 22). 2. Mother of King Rehoboam (I Kings xiv. 21).

NAAMAN—1. Fifth son of Benjamin (Gen. xlvi. 21). 2. A Benjamite, son of Bela (Num. xxvi. 40). 3. Commander-in-chief of the Syrian army in the days of Elisha; a good man and honourable; was stricken with leprosy and through the suggestion of a "little maid of the land of Israel," was induced to visit Elisha, who cured him (*see* the story in II Kings v.)

NAARAH—one of the wives of Ashur (I Chron. iv. 5).

NAARAI—a son of Esbai; one of David's valiant men (I Chron. xi. 37).

NABAL—a resident in Maon with possessions round Carmel. He returned a churlish answer to David when that monarch requested help for himself and his followers. He was saved from condign punishment by the tact of his wife, Abigail (I Sam. xxv. 1-42).

NABOTH—an inhabitant of Jezreel who refused to sell his birthright to Ahab when requested to do so. Through the intrigues of Jezebel he was put to death unjustly and Ahab then seized the inheritance (I Kings xxi. 1-24).

NACHOR—*see* Nahor.

NADAB—1. Eldest son of Aaron; he was appoint

to the priesthood ; with his brother he was consumed by fire for offering " strange fire " upon the altar (Num. iii. 4). 2. Son of Shammai of Judah (I Chron. ii. 28). 3. A Benjamite, son of Gibeon (I Chron. viii. 30). 4. Son and successor of Jeroboam (I Kings xiv. 20).

NAGGE—son of Maath (Luke iii. 25).

NAHAMANI—one who returned with Zerubbabel (Neh. vii. 7).

NAHARI—Joab's armour-bearer (II Sam. xxiii. 37).

NAHASH — 1. One of the parents of Abigail, Zeruiah's sister (II Sam. xvii. 25). 2. An Ammonite king who besieged Jabesh-gilead, but was defeated by the intervention of Saul, newly elected king (II Sam. x. 2).

NAHATH—a Kohathite Levite (I Chron. vi. 26)

NAHBI—the representative spy from the tribe of Naphtali (Num. xiii. 14).

NAHOR (Equivalent, NACHOR)—1. A son of Serug, and grandfather of Abraham (Gen. xi. 24). 2. A brother of Abraham (Gen. xi. 27).

NAHUM—a prophet, born at Elkosh. Practically nothing is known of his history (see his Book).

NAOMI—wife of Elimelech and mother of Mahlon and Chilion. (The whole story of her life may be read in the Book of Ruth).

NAPHTALI—sixth son of Jacob; described by his father as "a hind let loose ; he giveth goodly words " (Gen. xlix. 21).

NAPHTUHIM—a son of Mizraim ; or the term may refer to a tribe of Egyptian descent (Gen. x. 13).

NARCISSUS—a Christian at Rome to whom Paul sent salutations (Rom. xvi. 11).

NATHAN—a famous prophet in David's reign, who taught David the Lord's will with regard to the building of the temple, and and also showed him the reality of his sin with regard to Uriah the Hittite. (I Chron. xvii. 1-15) There are six other men of this name mentioned. See I Chron. ii. 36 ; II Sam. xxiii. 36 ; II Sam. v. 14 ; I Kings iv. 5 ; Ezra viii. 16 ; Ezra x. 39.

NATHANAEL—a native of Cana of Galilee, described by Christ as " an Israelite indeed, in whom is no guile." Probably the same person as Bartholomew (John i. 45).

NAUM—son of Esli and father of Amos (Luke iii. 25).

NEARIAH—1. A Simeonite who fought against the Amalekites (I Chron. iv. 42). 2. A descendant of King Jeconiah (I Chron. iii. 22).

NEBAI—one of the chief people with Nehemiah (Neh. x. 19).

NEBAT—father of Jeroboam I (I Kings xi. 26).

NEBUCHADNEZZAR (often spelt NEBUCHA-DREZZAR)—the Babylonian king in whose reign

Daniel was carried to Babylon. (*See* the story of Daniel and his friends and their treatment under this and other monarchs in the opening chapters of the Book of *Daniel*).

NEBUSHASBAN — a high Babylonian officer who took Jeremiah from the dungeon to which he had been consigned by his countrymen (Jer. xxxix. 13).

NEBUZAR-ADAN—captain of the guard in the army of Nebuchadnezzar at the capture of Jerusalem. It was he who burnt Solomon's temple and other valued buildings (II Kings xxv. 8-11).

NECHOH (also variously called NECOH, NECHO, —king of Egypt, whom Josiah encountered in battle at Megiddo when that king (Josiah) was mortally wounded. In Josiah's place he set up Jehoiakim as a puppet king. Later he was totally defeated by Nebuchadrezzar at Carchemish, the northern Hittite capital (II Kings xxiii. 29).

NEDABIAH—youngest son of King Jeconiah (I Chron. iii. 18).

NEHEMIAH—1. One of the chief men who returned with Zerubbabel (Ezra ii. 2). 2. An illustrious son of Hachaliah. He was one of the cup-bearers to Artaxerxes Longimanus at Shushan the Palace in Persia. Having heard from fugitive travellers the sad plight of Jerusalem, he sought and gained permission from the King to go with a party to rebuild the walls of the city. He met with many difficulties, and much opposition from neighbouring tribes, but ultimately carried the work to a successful conclusion, instigating a religious reform in the city. The story of his work is told graphically in the Book which bears his name.

NEHUM—one who returned with Zerubbabel (Neh. vii. 7).

NEHUSHTA—daughter of Elnathan of Jerusalem, and afterwards wife of King Jehoiakim (II Kings xxiv. 8).

NEKODA—founder of a family of Nethinim (Ezra ii. 48).

NEMUEL—same as JEMUEL (which *see*).

NEPHEG—1. Uncle of Aaron and Moses (Ex. vi. 21). 2. One of David's sons (II Sam. v. 15).

NEPHISH—eleventh son of Ishmael (I Chron. v. 19).

NER—a son of Abiel or Jehiel; father of Abner (I Sam. xiv. 50).

NEREUS—a Roman Christian saluted by Paul (Rom. xvi. 15).

NERI—son of Melchi (Luke iii. 27).

NERIAH—son of Maaseiah (Jer. xxxii. 12).

NETHANEEL—ten men of this name occur. *See* Num. i. 8; I Chron. ii. 14; I Chron. xv. 24; I Chron. xxiv. 6; I Chron. xxvi. 4; II Chron. xvii. 7; II Chron. xxxv. 9;

Ezra x. 22 ; Neh. xii. 21 ; Neh. xii. 36.

NETHANIAH—Four men bearing this name are mentioned (*see* I Chron. xxv. 2 ; II Chron. xvii. 8 ; Jer. xxxvi. 14 ; II Kings xxv. 23).

NEZIAH—founder of a family of Nethinim (Ezra ii. 54).

NICANOR—one of the seven original deacons (Acts vi. 5).

NICODEMUS—a ruler of the Jews who came to Jesus by night to enquire into His teaching. He appears to have spoken in favour of Christ in the Sanhedrin, and finally brought ointment to anoint Christ's body (John iii. 1).

NICOLAS—a proselyte of Antioch, one of the seven original deacons(Acts vi. 5).

NIMROD—a son of Cush ; described as "a mighty hunter before the Lord" (Gen. x. 8).

NIMSHI—grandfather of Jehu (I Kings xix. 16).

NOADIAH—1. Son of Binnui. One of those who took charge of the gold and silver vessels the returned captives and Ezra brought back to Jerusalem (Ezra viii. 33). 2. An evil prophetess who tried to frighten Nehemiah (Neh. vi. 14).

NOAH—eldest son of Lamech ; a just man and one who "walked with God." God intimated to him that He would destroy the corrupt age by a flood, and so Noah became a "preacher of righteousness." His

warnings, however, were ignored, and so God instructed him to build an ark. He was to take with him into this ark specimens of all types of animal life, so as to preserve life upon the earth after the deluge had destroyed those who had persistently ignored God's warning. He lived on after the Flood for many years, and was the vehicle of some precious promises of God, though he was not altogether sinless in his way of life (*read* from Gen. vi. 5, onwards).

NOBAH—a Manassite warrior (Num. xxxii. 42).

NOGAH—a son of David (I Chron. iii. 7).

NOHAH—fourth son of Benjamin (I Chron. viii. 2).

NUN—the father of Joshua (Ex. xxxiii. 11).

O

OBADIAH—1. Son of Israhiah (I Chron. vii. 3). 2. One of David's Gadite heroes (I Chron. xii. 9). 3. A Zebulonite chief in David's reign (I Chron. xxvii. 19). 4. A descendant of Jonathan (I Chron. viii. 38). 5. The governor of Ahab's palace and a prominent man during the period of Elijah's prophecies (I Kings xviii. 3). 6. A prince in the days of Jehoshaphat (II Chron. xvii. 7). 7. An overseer of the Temple in Josiah's reign (II Chron. xxiv. 12). 8. The author of the Book of *Obadiah*. Practically nothing is known of his personal life (*see* his Book). 9. A descendant of King Jeconiah (I Chron. iii. 21). 10. A son of Jehiel (Ezra viii. 9). 11. A priest with Nehemiah (Neh. x. 5). 12. A Levite porter (Neh. xii. 25).

OBAL—eighth son of Joktan (Gen. x. 28).

OBED—there are five men of this name in Scripture, none of whom is outstanding (*see* I Chron. ii. 37; Ruth iv. 17; I Chron. xi. 47; I Chron. xxvi. 7; II Chron. xiii. 1).

OBED-EDOM—1. Sheltered the ark in his home for three months and received many blessings in consequence (II Sam. vi. 10-12). 2. A Levite porter in David's reign (II Chron. xxv. 24).

O B I L—an Ishmaelite in charge of David's camels (I Chron. xxvii. 30).

OCRAN—father of Pagiel (Num. i. 13).

ODED—1. Father of the prophet Azariah (II Chron. xv. 1). 2. An Israelite prophet in the reign of Pekah. His message resulted in the northern kingdom returning Judean captives, after battle, in a specially brotherly fashion (II Chron. xxviii. 9).

OG—an Amorite king of Bashan; a giant notable for his big bed—about 13½ feet by 6 feet—(Num. xxi. 33).

OHAD—third son of Simeon (Gen. xlvi. 10).

OHEL—a son of Zerubbabel (I Chron. iii. 20).

OMAR—second son of Eliphaz (Gen. xxxvi. 11).

OMRI—1. Grandson of Benjamin (I Chron. vii. 8). 2. A son of Imri (I Chron. ix. 4). 3. A son of Michael in David's reign (I Chron. xxvii. 18). 4. One of the kings of Israel. The chief event of his reign was the founding of a new capital at Samaria (I Kings xvi. 23).

ON—a Reubenite chief who took part in Korah's rebellion against Moses (Num. xvi. 1).

ONAM—1. A Horite, son of Shobal (Gen. xxxvi. 23). 2. A son of Jerahmeel (I Chron. ii. 26).

ONAN—a son of Judah (Gen. xxxviii. 4-10).

ONESIMUS—a slave belonging to Philemon, Paul's friend. He escaped to Rome, where he was converted by Paul and returned home bearing a letter from Paul to Philemon recommending him to his master's kindly consideration. With Tychicus, he bore Paul's Epistle to the Colossians (Philemon 10-19; Col. iv. 7-9).

ONESIPHORUS—a Christian who sought out Paul at Rome (II Tim. i. 16).

OPHRAH—a son of Menothai, of the tribe of Judah (I Chron. iv. 14).

OREB—one of two Midianite princes, defeated, captured and put to death by Gideon (Judg. vii. 25).

OREN—a son of Jerahmeel (I Chron. ii. 25).

ORPAH—the wife of Mah-

lon, and the sister-in-law of Ruth (Ruth i. 4).

OSHEA—*see* Joshua.

OTHNI—a porter, son of Shemaiah (I Chron. xxvi. 7).

OTHNIEL—son of Kenaz, Caleb's brother (I Chron. iv. 13).

OZEM—1. Sixth son of Jesse (I Chron. ii. 15). 2. A son of Jerahmeel (I Chron. ii. 25).

OZNI—a son of Gad, and founder of the family of the Oznites (Num. xxvi. 16).

P

PADON—the founder of a family of Nethinim (Ezra ii. 44).

PAGIEL—head of the Asherite tribe in the wilderness (Num. i. 13).

PALAL—son of Uzai, who took part in building the wall with Nehemiah (Neh. iii. 25).

PALTI—the representative spy from the tribe of Benjamin (Num. xiii. 9).

PALTIEL—a prince over the tribe of Issachar (Num. xxxiv. 26).

PARMASHTA — a son of Haman (Esther ix. 9).

PARMENAS—one of the original " seven deacons " (Acts vi. 5).

PARNACH—a Zebulunite ; father of prince Elizaphan (Num. xxxiv. 25).

PARUAH—the father of a certain Jehoshaphat (I Kings iv. 17).

PASEAH—1. Son of Eshton (I Chron. iv. 12). 2. Fa-

ther of a certain Jehoida (Ezra ii. 49).

PASHHUR (also spelt PASHUR)—four men of this name are mentioned, as follows : Jer. xxi. 1 ; Jer. xx. 1-6 ; Jer. xxxviii. 1 ; Ezra x. 22.

PATROBAS—a Christian at Rome to whom Paul sent his salutations (Rom. xvi. 14).

PAUL—next to Jesus Christ, the best-known and most outstanding character of the New Testament. Born at Tarsus and educated partly there and partly at Jerusalem, he became familiar with the thoughts of both Jew and Gentile. He was a member of the Sanhedrin, and the highest positions of his race seemed open to him. He fiercely persecuted the Christians until, gaining letters to justify his zealous work being done further afield, he set off for Damascus. He had recently witnessed the death of Stephen and in his lonely journey to Damascus at the head of his troops he seems to have thought very keenly about the things that Stephen stood for. As he drew near to Damascus he was granted a vision, and the result was that Jesus spoke to him and all was changed. At first he was mistrusted by the Church, who thought this merely some new ruse for persecuting them. Barnabas, however, brought him forward, and he began upon his life-long work of evangelising Asia

Minor, going even into Europe. Possibly no leader of the Church has had more influence upon Christian thought. He went on several famous missionary journeys, and finally went as a prisoner to Rome, where we lose sight of him. It is generally supposed that he died for his faith. He left a valuable legacy of writings (*see* Acts vii. 58, and onward through the whole of that Book, as well as the Epistles that bear his name) (Acts vii. 58, etc.).

PEDAHEL—a prince of the tribe of Naphtali in the wilderness (Num. xxxiv. 28).

PEDAHZUR—father of Gamaliel, prince of the tribe of Manasseh in the wilderness (Num. i. 10).

PEDAIAH—1. Father of a certain Joel in the reign of David (I Chron. xxvii. 20). 2. Father of Zebudah (II Kings xxiii. 36). 3. Son of Salathiel, and grandson of King Jeconiah (I Chron. iii. 18, 19). Other men of like name are mentioned in Neh. iii. 25 ; Neh. viii. 4 ; Neh. xi. 7 ; Neh. xiii. 13.

PEKAH—the son of Remaliah ; king of the northern kingdom. He practised calf-worship, and also entered into an alliance with Rezin, king of Syria. Together they invaded Judah and wrought much havoc. Being attacked, however, by Tiglath-pileser of Assyria, their own land was devastated. Pekah was assassinated by Hoshea, son of Elah, who afterwards ascended the throne (II Kings xv. 25-28, etc.).

PEKAHIAH—son and successor of Menahem in the kingdom of Israel. Ultimately assassinated in his palace at Samaria by a captain of his, Pekah—*see* above (II Kings xv. 23-26).

PELAIAH—1. A Levite with Ezra (Neh. viii. 7). 2. Third son of Elioenai, a descendant of King Jeconiah (I Chron. iii. 24.).

PELALIAH—a priest, father of Jeroham (Neh. xi. 12).

PELATIAH—four men of this name are mentioned as follows : I Chron. iv. 42 ; Ezek. xi. 1-13 ; Neh. x. 22; I Chron. iii. 21.

PELEG—elder son of Ebur and father of Reu (Gen. xi. 16-19).

PELET—son of Jahdai (I Chron. ii. 47).

PELETH—a man of Judah (I Chron. ii. 33).

PENINNAH—one of Elkanah's two wives (I Sam. i. 2-6).

PERESH—a son of Machir (I Chron. vii. 16).

PERSIS—a Christian at Rome (Rom. xvi. 12).

PETER—an eminent Apostle of Jesus Christ ; originally called Cephas. One of the chosen three, and therefore intimate with his Lord in some of Christ's most precious moments. He was called from the fishing nets to follow Christ. Was of volatile disposition, always meaning well, yet showing signs of over-exuberance of spirit at times. He was

with his Master in the Garden on the betrayal night, and when the rest " forsook Him and fled," Peter followed afar off, later in the night denying thrice that he knew Jesus, but afterwards regretting his weakness. He was among the earliest at the tomb on the Resurrection morning, and showed no weakness when he charged the Jews to the teeth with the slaying of Christ. He took a prominent place in the work of the early Church. Was imprisoned for his faith, but was miraculously released. He appears to have died a martyr's death, being, according to tradition, crucified head downwards. He wrote two Epistles which have survived (*see* John i. 42, and many other passages both in the Gospels and in the *Acts*. *Equivalent*, Bar-jona.

PETHAHIAH—three men of this name are mentioned, all Levites (*see* I Chron. xxiv. 16; Ezra x. 23; Neh. xi. 24.

PETHUEL—father of the prophet Joel (Joel i. 1).

PEULTHAI—a Korhite porter (I Chron. xxvi. 5).

PHANUEL—an Asherite, father of Anna (Luke ii. 36).

PHARAOH—an official name given to the kings of Egypt, and therefore we read of many men who bore that name during the period of the Old Testament. Different holders of the title met with Abraham

(Gen. xii. 10-20); the Pharaoh of Joseph (Gen. xxxix. ff.); the one who oppressed the Israelites in bondage in Egypt (Ex. i. 11); one was Hadad's brother-in-law; another was father-in-law to Solomon (I Kings iii. 1); and there are others of later years, including Pharaohnechoh (II Kings, xxiii. 29).

PHAREZ—a son of Judah (Gen. xxxviii. 27-30).

PHEBE—a deaconess of the Church at Cenchrea (Rom. xvi. 1, 2).

PHICOL—chief captain of the army belonging to Abimelech (Gen. xxi. 22).

PHILEMON—a convert of Paul's in Colosse. His runaway slave, Onesimus, was helpful to Paul in Rome, and Paul wrote the Epistle to Philemon to ask clemency for this helper (*see* the whole Epistle).

PHILETUS—a leading heretic (II Tim. ii. 17, 18).

PHILIP—1. Son of Herod and rightful husband of Herodias (Matt. xiv. 3). 2. Philip the Tetrarch another son of Herod the Great (Luke iii. 1). 3 Philip the Apostle (Matt. x. 3); 4. Philip the Evangelist, one of the original seven deacons, who did much evangelistic work in Samaria, on the road to Gaza, and at Azotus (Acts vi. 5).

PHILOLOGUS—a Roman Christian to whom Paul sent salutations (Rom. xvi. 15).

PHINEHAS—1. Son of Eleazar, and grandson of

Aaron. He slew an Israelite who had brought a Midianitish woman into the camp, and so stayed a plague. He was promised for his family an everlasting priesthood (Ex. vi. 25). 2. The younger of Eli's two degenerate sons, who was killed in battle with the Philistines, when the ark had been sacrilegiously taken into battle (I Sam. i. 3). 3. The father of a certain Eleazar (Ezra viii. 33).

PHURAH—a servant of Gideon's who went with him by night to reconnoitre the Midianite camp (Judg. vii. 10, 11).

PHUT—third son of Ham (Gen. x. 6).

PHYGELLUS—a Christian in Asia who turned away from Paul (II Tim. i. 15).

PILATE—also called Pontius Pilate, sixth Roman Procurator in Judæa, appointed by Tiberius Cæsar; had caused a massacre of the Jews (Luke xiii. 1); chiefly remembered because Christ "suffered under Pontius Pilate." It is believed that Pilate was ultimately banished to Vienne in France and that he committed suicide.

PILDASH—a son of Bethuel and Milcah (Gen. xxii. 22).

PILEHA—one who was with Nehemiah (Neh. x. 24).

PILTAI—a priest of the family of Moadiah (Neh. xii. 17).

PINON—a duke of Edom (Gen. xxxvi. 41).

PIRAM—a Canaanite king of Jarmuth (Josh. x. 3).

PISPAH—an Asherite, son of Jether (I Chron. vii. 38).

PITHON—son of a certain Micah (I Chron. viii. 35).

POCHERETH—founder of a family who returned from Babylon (Ezra ii. 57).

PONTIUS PILATE—*see* Pilate.

PORATHA—one of Haman's sons (Esther ix. 8).

POTIPHAR—captain of Pharaoh's guard, into whose house Joseph went (Gen. xxxix. 1-20).

POTI-PHERA—a priest of On, or Heliopolas (Gen. xli. 45).

PRISCILLA—wife of Aquila (which *see*).

PROCHORUS—one of the original seven deacons (Acts vi. 5).

PUAH—second son of Issachar (I Chron. vii. 1).

PUBLIUS—the chief man in the island of Melita (Malta) while Paul was there (Acts xxviii. 8).

PUDENS—a Christian at Rome who joined Paul in sending salutations to Timothy (II Timothy iv. 21).

PUL—a king of Assyria (II Kings xv. 19).

PUTIEL—father of Pharaoh's wife (Ex. vi. 25).

PUVAH — 1. Son of Issachar (Gen. xlvi. 13). 2. A man belonging to the tribe of Issachar (Judg. x. 1). There are four forms of this name, viz.— Puvah, Phuvah, Pua, Puah.

Q

QUARTUS—a Corinthian Christian who joined Paul

in sending a salutation to the Church at Rome (Rom. xvi. 23).

QUIRINIUS—another form of Cyrenius—a Roman who became governor of Syria after the deposition of Archelaus, A.D. 6 (Luke ii. 2).

R

RAAMAH—fourth son of Cush (Gen. x. 7).

RAB-SHAKEH—the official title of Sennacherib's representative who came to urge surrender upon Jerusalem at the time of the Assyrian siege (Isaiah xxxvi. 2, etc.).

RACHEL—youngest daughter of Laban, who was possessed of great personal beauty. Jacob afterwards married her and she became the mother of Joseph and Benjamin, the latter of whom cost her her life (Gen. xxix. 1-30).

RADDAI—fifth son of Jesse and brother of King David (I Chron. ii. 14).

RAHAB—known as "the harlot." The spies sent by Joshua to the promised land took shelter in her house, which was spared, together with her life, when Jericho was besieged (Josh. ii. 1-24).

RAHAM—son of Shema, one of Caleb's descendants (I Chron. ii. 44).

RAKEM—a Manassite, son of Sheresh (I Chron. vii. 16).

RAM—three men of this name are mentioned in Scripture (see Ruth iv.

19; I Chron. ii. 25; Job xxxii. 2).

RAMIAH—son of Parosh (Ezra x. 25).

RAMOTH—son of Bani (Ezra x. 29).

RAPHA—a descendant of Jonathan (I Chron. viii. 37).

REAIAH (or REAIA)—three men of this name are mentioned (see I Chron. iv. 2; I Chron. v. 5; Ezra. ii. 47).

REBA—a Midianite king defeated and slain by Israel in the time of Moses (Num. xxxi. 8).

REBEKAH—a daughter of Bethuel, who became the wife of Isaac. The whole story of how this was brought about can be read at length in Gen. xxiv. 1-67.

RECHAB—1. Son of Rimmon; captain of a band under Ish-bosheth (II Sam. iv. 2). 2. Father of Jehonadab (II Kings x. 15). 3. Father of Malchiah (Neh. iii. 14).

REELAIAH—one of the leading men who accompanied Zerubbabel (Ezra ii. 2).

REGEM—son of Jahdai, descendant of Caleb (I Chron. ii. 47).

REHOB—1. Father of Hadadezer (II Sam. viii. 3, 12). 2. A Levite with Nehemiah (Neh. x. 11).

REHOBOAM—son of Solomon by Naamah. Headstrong and short-sighted as a ruler. As a result of his unwillingness to lighten the people's burdens the kingdom became divided,

Jeroboam ruling over one half (*read* I Kings xii, 1, etc.).

REHUM—there are four of this name (*see* Ezra iv. 8 ; Ezra ii. 2 ; Neh. x. 25 ; Neh. iii. 17).

REI—a Jewish dignitary who refused to join Adonijah in his usurpation (I Kings i. 8).

REKEM—1. King of Midian (Num. xxxi. 8). 2. Descendant of Caleb (I Chron. ii. 43).

REMALIAH—father of Pekah (II Kings xv. 25).

REPHAEL—second son of Shemaiah (I Chron. xxvi. 7).

REPHAH—an Ephraimite, ancestor of Joshua (I Chron. vii. 25).

REPHAIAH—the name of five men as follows : I Chron. vii. 2 ; I Chron. ix. 43 ; I Chron. iv. 42 ; Neh. iii. 9 ; I Chron. iii. 21.

RESHEPH—a son of Ephraim (I Chron. vii. 25).

REU—a son of Peleg (Gen. xi. 18).

REUBEN—Jacob's eldest son, guilty of gross misconduct, yet when Joseph was being ill-treated by his brethren Reuben tried to save him. " Unstable as water," yet with many good points (Gen. xxix. 31-32).

REUEL—1. Son of Esau (Gen. xxxvi. 4). 2. A name given to Moses' father-in-law (Ex. ii. 18). 3. A Benjamite (I Chron. ix. 8). 4. The father of Eliasaph (Num. ii. 14).

REZIA—*see* Rizia.

REZIN—a king of Syria,

confederate with Pekah (*see* Isaiah vii. 1 to ix. 12).

REZON—a son of Eliadah, founded the kingdom of Damascus during David's time (I Kings xi. 23-25).

RHESA—son of Zerubbabel (Luke iii. 27).

RHODA—a servant girl of Mary the mother of Mark. Answered the door when Peter was delivered from prison, but refused through sheer excitement to admit him for a time (Acts. xii. 13-16).

RIBAI—a Benjamite of Gibeah, father of Ittai who was one of David's mighty men (II Sam. xxiii. 29).

RIMMON—his two sons were captains under Ish-bosheth (II Sam. iv. 2).

RIMMON—different derivation from preceding—a Syrian god, in whose temple Naaman and his royal master bowed down (II Kings v. 18).

RINNAH—a man of Judah (I Chron. iv. 20).

RIPHATH—second son of Gomer (Gen. x. 3).

RIZIA or REZIA—an Asherite, son of Ulla (I Chron. vii. 39).

RIZPAH—a concubine of Saul (II Sam. iii. 6-8).

ROHGAH—an Asherite son of Shamer (I Chron. vii. 34).

ROMAMTI-EZER–a singer, son of Heman (I Chron. xxv. 4).

ROSH—a son of Benjamin (Gen. xlvi. 21).

RUFUS—younger son of Simon of Cyrene, who was compelled to bear the cross for Christ (Mark xv. 21).

RUTH—a Moabitess, mar-

ried first to Mahlon, son
of Naomi, and ultimately
to Boaz. The whole story
of her life is very beautiful
and should be read at
length in the Book of
Ruth.

S

SABTAH—third son of Cush
(Gen. x. 7).
SABTECA—also called Sab-
techa, etc. ; fifth son of
Cush (Gen. x. 7).
SACAR—1. Father of Ahiam
(I Chron. xi. 35).   2.
Fourth son of Obed-edom
(I Chron. xxvi. 4).
SADOC—son of Azor (Matt.
i. 14).
SALAH—son of Arphaxad
(Gen. x. 24).
SALLAI — 1. A Benjamite
who consented to reside at
Jerusalem (Neh. xi. 8).   2.
A priest who came from
Babylon with Zerubbabel
(Neh. xii. 20).
SALMON—the   son   of
Nahshon and father of
Boaz (Ruth iv. 20).
SALOME—wife of Zebedee
and mother of James and
John the Apostles.   She
asked Jesus for chief pla-
ces for her sons.   She was
one of those who went to
the sepulchre on the morn-
ing of the Resurrection.
(Mark xv. 40).
SALU—a leader in the tribe
of Simeon (Num. xxv. 14).
SAMGAR-NEBO—one of
Nebuchadrezzar's princes
(Jer. xxxix. 3).
SAMLAH—a king of the
Edomites (Gen. xxxvi. 36).
SAMSON—one of the most
eminent of the Hebrew
judges ; born at Zora and

was a Nazarite from birth.
Notorious for his strength,
and in some ways similar
to the Hercules of heathen
mythology.   He   married
a heathen wife, Delilah,
by whom he was betrayed.
She learnt that the secret
of his strength lay in his
Nazarite vow, and secured
the breaking of these.
Blinded and led captive,
he was present as an object
of ridicule at the festival
of the fish-god Dagon.   In
answer to his prayer re-
newed strength was given
to him, so that he brought
great destruction upon all
at the festival, thus slaying
a host in his death (Judg.
xiii. 1-24).
SAMUEL—earliest of the
greater Hebrew prophets.
Was dedicated to the ser-
vice of the Temple as a
child and attended upon
Eli.   Tried to preserve the
nation as a Theocracy
(governed by God alone),
but ultimately yielded to
the desire for a king.   He
adopted vigorous methods
towards the foes of his
nation, though these
seemed justified by results.
In his old age he made his
two sons judges at Beer-
sheba, but they proved
unworthy of the trust
(*see* the whole of the
First Book of *Samuel* for
the story of his work).
SANBALLAT—a Horonite
and provincial governor
under Artaxerxes Longi-
manus.   He did his best
to hinder the work of
Nehemiah, but was foiled
in his plots.   He built the

Samaritan temple on Mount Gerizim (Neh. iv. 1, etc.).

SAPH—a Philistine giant (II Sam. xxi. 18).

SAPPHIRA—the wife of that Ananias who, like herself, was struck dead in the days of the Apostolic Church for " lying to the Holy Ghost" by keeping back part of the price of the land they sold (Acts v. 1-11).

SARAH—the later name of SARAI, the wife of Abraham. Abraham married her in Ur of the Chaldees. She accompanied him on all his journeys in the great migration he undertook, going to Egypt with him, where he practised deception to save her, as he thought, though it was made plain to him that such conduct was more productive of evil than of good, for Pharaoh rebuked him. When all hope of a son seemed past Isaac was born to her, and brought great joy to the home. She died at Kirjath-Arba (Hebron) at the age of 127, and was buried in the cave of Machpelah (Gen. xi. 28-31).

SARAPH—a descendant of Shelah (I Chron. iv. 22).

SARGON—a famous Assyrian king mentioned only once in Scripture (Isaiah xx. 1).

SARSECHIM—one of Nebuchadnezzar's princes (Jer. xxxix. 3).

SATAN—the adversary— and accuser. Stands generally for the Devil, (which see), but at times, as in the Book of *Job*, has a distinctive character as an evil spirit who accuses Job to the Almighty (see Zech. iii. I and Job i. 6-22).

SAUL—the first king of Israel, a tall strong man, who appeared to promise well, but who fell into pride and disobedience on several occasions. In consequence of his sin he was "rejected" from being king over Israel, and David was anointed as his successor. On several occasions he sought to take David's life, but was unsuccessful. He reigned about forty years over his nation. (I Sam. ix. 2).

SAVIOUR—one of the names for Jesus (which see). The word " Jesus " is from a root meaning "saviour," and is in correspondence with the Hebrew word " Joshua," which has the same meaning (Luke ii. 11, etc). God the Father is also spoken of in certain passages as " Saviour" (Luke i. 4, 47).

SCEVA—a Jew who had been high priest and whose seven sons were exorcists (Acts xix. 14).

SEBA—the eldest son of Cush (Gen. x. 7).

SECUNDUS—a companion of Paul (Acts. xx. 4).

SEIR—a Horite, or cave-dweller (I Chron. i. 38).

SELED—a son of Nadab (I Chron. ii. 30).

SEMACHIAH—a son of Shemaiah and grandson of Obed-edom (I Chron. xxvi. 7).

SEMEI—father of Matta-
thias (Luke iii. 26).

SENNACHERIB—a youn-
ger son of Sargon, suc-
ceeded his father as king of
Assyria.   He was boastful
and cruel, and not a wise
ruler.   The most notable
Biblical episode connected
with his name was that
famous threat to Jerusa-
lem, when, after laying
most of the district waste,
he sent his Rabshakeh, or
prime minister, to overawe
little Jerusalem.   Under
the guidance of Isaiah,
Hezekiah defied him, and
by a mysterious stroke of
God the army posted
around Jerusalem pe-
rished in a night (see
Isaiah xxxvi-xxxix, and
the corresponding narra-
tives in II Kings xviii-xx
and II Chron. xxxii. 1-
33).

SEORIM—the head of a
course of priests in David's
time (I Chron. xxiv. 8).

SERAH—a daughter of
Asher (Gen. xlvi. 17).

SERAIAH—there are twelve
of this name in Scripture
The following are the
references : I Chron. iv.
13 ; II Sam. viii. 17 ; I
Chron. iv. 35 ; Jer. xxxvi.
26 ; I Chron. iv. 14 ; Jer.
li. 59 ; Jer. xl. 8 ; Ezra
vii. 1 ; Ezra ii. 2 ; Neh.
xii. 1 (possibly same as
Ezra vii. 1) ; Neh. x. 2 ; Neh.
xi. 11).

SERED—eldest son of
Zebulun (Gen. xlvi. 14).

SERGIUS PAULUS—pro-
consul of Cyprus, con-
verted by Paul (Acts. xiii.
5-12).

SERUG—son of Reu ; father
of Nahor (Gen. xi. 20).

SETH—third son of Adam,
born after the murder of
Abel, for whom to some
extent he became a substi-
tute (Gen. iv. 25).

SETHUR—the representa-
tive spy from the tribe of
Asher (Num. xiii. 13).

SHAAPH—son of Jahdai, a
descendant of Caleb (I
Chron. ii. 47).

SHAASHGAZ—a chamber-
lain of King Ahasuerus (Esther ii. 14).

SHABBETHAI — a Levite
who assisted Ezra (Ezra
x. 15).

SHACHIA—a Benjamite,
son of Shaharaim (I Chron.
viii. 10).

SHADRACH—one of Da-
niel's companions (Dan. i.
7).

SHAGE—a Hararite, father
of one of David's mighty
men (I Chron. xi. 34).

SHAHARAIM—a Benja-
mite, chiefly famous be-
cause of his descendants
(I Chron. viii. 8).

SHALLUM—there are fif-
teen people of this name
in Scripture, the following
are the references : I Chron.
vii. 13 ; I Chron. iv. 25 ;
I Chron. ii. 40 ; I Chron.
ix. 17—? same man in v.
19 of this chapter ; II
Kings xv. 10 ; II Chron.
xxviii. 12 ; I Chron. vi.
12 ; II Chron. xxxiv. 22 ;
Jer. xxxii. 7 (may pos-
sibly be same as preceding
name) ; Jer. xxxv. 4 ; I
Chron. iii. 15 ; Ezra x.
24 ; Ezra x. 42 ; Neh. iii.
12.

SHALLUN—a ruler of part of Mizpah (Neh. iii. 15).

SHALMAI—founder of a family of the Nethinim (Ezra ii. 46).

SHALMANESER (or SHALMAN)—this is the name of four Assyrian kings ; their dates have been given approximately as : (1) 1300-1271 B.C.; (2) 860-825 B.C.; (3) 783-773 B.C. ; (4) 727-722 B.C. (Kings xvii. 3).

SHAMA—a son of Hothan (I Chron. xi. 44).

SHAMED—son of Elpaal; one of the builders of Ono and Lod (I Chron. viii. 12).

SHAMGAR—a Hebrew judge, son of Anak ; slew 600 of the Philistines with an ox-goad, and thus delivered Israel. His date is uncertain (Judg. iii. 31).

SHAMHUTH—one of David's captains (I Chron. xxvii. 8).

SHAMIR—a Levite, son of Michah (I Chron. xxiv. 24).

SHAMMAH — 1. A son of Reuel (Gen. xxxvi. 13). 2. Third son of Jesse (I Sam. xvi. 9). 3. One of David's three mighty men (II Sam. xxiii. 33). 4. Another of David's mighty men (II Sam. xxiii. 33). 5. A Harodite (II Sam. xxiii. 25).

SHAMMAI — 1. A son of Onam (I Chron. ii. 28). 2. A son of Rekem (I Chron. ii. 44). 3. Son of a certain Ezra (I Chron. iv. 17).

SHAMMUA — 1. Reuben's representative spy (Num. xiii. 4). 2. A son of David (II Sam. v. 14). 3. A Levite, son of Galal (Neh. xi. 17). 4. A priest in the days of Joiakim (Neh. xii. 18).

SHAMSHERAI — a Benjamite, son of Jeroham (I Chron. viii. 26).

SHAPHAM—second man of the tribe of Gad (I Chron. v. 12).

SHAPHAN—a noted scribe in the days of Josiah. He read the "Book of the Law" to the king (II Kings xxii. 8-14).

SHAPHAT—there are four men of this name, all unimportant, the references are as follows : Num. xiii. 5 ; I Chron. v. 12 ; I Chron. xxvii. 29 ; I Kings xix. 16; I Chron. iii. 22.

SHARAI—a " son " of Bani (Ezra x. 40)

SHARAR—father of Ahiam (II Sam. xxiii. 33).

SHAREZER—1. Son of Sennacherib, whom he helped to murder (II Kings xix. 37). 2. A Jew in Zechariah's time (Zech. vii. 2).

SHASHAI—son of Bani (Ezra x. 40).

SHASHAK—a Benjamite, a son of Elpaal (I Chron. viii. 14).

SHAUL—a son of Simeon by a Canaanitish woman (Gen. xlvi. 10).

SHAVSHA—one of David's scribes (I Chron. xviii. 16).

SHEAL—a son of Bani (Ezra x. 29).

SHEALTIEL—father of Zerubbabel (Ezra iii. 2).

SHEARIAH—a son of Azel, a descendant of Jonathan (I Chron. viii. 38).

SHEAR-JASHUB—a son of Isaiah ; the name is sym-

bolic and means " a remnant shall return " (Isaiah vii. 3).

SHEBA—1. A grandson of Cush (Gen. x. 7). 2. A son of Joktan (Gen. x. 28). 3. A grandson of Abraham by Keturah (Gen. xxv. 3). 4. A Benjamite, son of Bichri ; he led a rebellion against David, but was ultimately defeated and slain (II Sam. xx. 1-22).

SHEBANIAH—a Levite or possibly a priest who assisted Nehemiah (Neh. x. 4).

SHEBER—a son of Caleb (I Chron. ii. 48).

SHEBNA—a treasurer over the palace of Hezekiah. He was denounced by Isaiah and succeeded by Hilkiah (Isaiah xxii. 15-25).

SHEBUEL—a son of Gershom (I Chron. xxiii. 16).

SHECANIAH — 1. A priest in David's reign (I Chron. xxiv. 11). 2. A Levite in Hezekiah's reign (II Chron. xxxi. 15). 3. Head of a priestly family who returned with Zerubbabel (Neh. xii. 3). 4. Father-in-law of Tobiah the Ammonite (Neh. vi. 18).

SHECHEM—1. Son of Hamor the Hivite (Gen. xxxiv. 2). 2. A son of Gilead and founder of the Shechemites (Num. xxvi. 31).

SHEDEUR—father of Elizur (Num. i. 5).

SHEHARIAH—son of Jeroham (I Chron. viii. 26).

SHELEMIAH — 1. A porter in David's time (I Chron. xxvi. 14). 2. Grandfather

of Jehudi (Jer. xxxvi. 14). 3. One of those sent to arrest Baruch and Jeremiah (Jer. xxxvi. 26). 4. Father of Hananiah (Neh. iii. 30). 5. A priest under Nehemiah (Neh. xiii. 13).

SHELEPH—a son of Joktan (Gen. x. 26).

SHELESH—an Asherite, son of Helem (I Chron. vii. 35).

SHELOMI—father of Ahihud (Num. xxxiv. 27).

SHELOMITH — 1. A Danite daughter of Dibri (Lev. xxiv. 11). 2. A Gershomite Levite (I Chron. xxiii. 18). 3. A child of Rehoboam (II Chron. xi. 20). 4. A daughter of Zerubbabel (I Chron. iii. 19).

SHELUMIEL—the prince of the tribe of Simeon in the wilderness wanderings (Num. i. 6).

SHEM—second son of Noah. Acted the part of a loyal and dutiful son in trying circumstances, and was consequently blessed. He had five children, Elam, Asshur, Arphaxad, Lud and Aram. These are regarded as the founders of the Elamites, the Assyrians, the Chaldeans, the Lydians and the Syrians (Gen. vii. 13).

SHEMA—a Benjamite : one of the heads of the village community of Aijalon (I Chron. viii. 13).

SHEMAIAH—about twenty-five Shemaiahs are mentioned in Scripture (see I Chron. iv. 37 ; I Chron. v. 4 ; I Chron. xv. 8 ; I Chron. xxiv. 6 ; I Chron. xxvi. 6 ; I Kings xii. 22 ;

II Chron. xvii. 8; II
Chron. xix. 14; II Chron.
xxxi. 15; II Chron. xxxv.
9; Jer. xxvi. 20; Jer.
xxxvi. 12; Jer. xxix. 24;
Neh. xii. 6; Ezra viii. 13;
Ezra viii. 16; Ezra x. 21;
Ezra x. 31; Neh. iii. 29;
Neh. xi. 15; Neh. vi. 10;
Neh. x. 8; Neh. xii. 34;
Neh. xii. 35; Neh. xii. 42).

SHEMARIAH—the name of
four men, all unimportant,
mentioned in I Chron. xii,
5; II Chron. xi. 19; Ezra
x. 32; Ezra x. 41.

SHEMEBER—king of Ze-
boiim, defeated by Abra-
ham (Gen. xiv. 2).

SHEMER—the original ow-
ner of the hill on which
Samaria was built (I Kings
xvi. 24).

SHEMIDA—a son of Gilead,
and founder of the Shemi-
daites (Num. xxvi. 32).

SHEMIRAMOTH—a Levite
and singer in David's time
(I Chron. xv. 18).

SHEMUEL—son of Ammi-
hud; a representative of
the tribe of Simeon in the
division of Canaan (Num.
xxxiv. 20).

SHENAZAR—son of Sala-
thiel (I Chron. iii. 18).

SHEPHATIAH—the name
occurs with reference to
nine men, none of whom is
at all prominent except the
son of Mattan mentioned in
Jer. xxxviii. 1. This man
advised Zedekiah to put
Jeremiah to death on
account of that prophet's
unfavourable prophecies.
The others are mentioned
in I Chron. xii. 5; II Sam.
iii. 4; I Chron. xxvii. 16;
I Chron. ix 8 (Variant,

Shephathiah); II Chron.
xxi. 2; Ezra viii. 8; Neh.
xi. 4; Ezra ii. 57.

SHEPHO—a son of Shobal
(Gen. xxxvi. 23).

SHEPHUPHAN—a son of
Bela (I Chron. viii. 5).

SHERAH—a daughter of
Ephraim (I Chron. vii. 24).

SHEREBIAH—a son of
Mahli; ·he shared the
custody of the temple vessels with Ezra (Ezra viii.
18).

SHERESH—a son of Machir
and grandson of Manasseh
(I Chron. vii. 16).

SHESHAI—a giant, son of
Anak, living at Hebron
(Num. xiii. 22).

SHESHAN—a son of Ishi of
the tribe of Judah (I
Chron. ii. 31).

SHESHBAZZAR—a prince
of Judah by whom Cyrus
restored the Temple ves-
sels carried to Babylon by
Nebuchadnezzar (Ezra i.
8).

SHETHAR-BOZNAI—a
Persian governor who at-
tempted to hinder the re-
turned exiles rebuilding
the Temple (Ezra v. 3).

SHEVA — 1. A son of Caleb
(I Chron. ii. 49). 2. A
scribe in David's reign
(II Sam. xx. 25).

SHILHI—father of Azubah,
Jehoshaphat's mother (I
Kings xxii. 42).

SHILLEM—a son of Naph-
tali and founder of the
Shillemites (Gen. xlvi. 24).

SHILSHAH—an Asherite,
son of Zophah (I Chron.
vii. 37).

SHIMEA—a brother of King
David (I Chron. xx. 7),
after whom David called

one of his sons (I Chron. iii. 5).

SHIMEAH — a Benjamite, son of Mikloth (I Chron. viii. 32).

SHIMEATH (SHIMI)— an Ammonitess, mother of Jozachar (II Kings xii. 21).

SHIMEI—1. Son of Gershom and grandson of Levi (Ex. vi. 17). 2. A Benjamite, son of Gera, who cursed David, but who professed penitence when David came to power again. He was ultimately put to death for disobeying Solomon's commands (II Sam. xvi. 5-14). 3. There are some sixteen further men so named (see the following references: I Chron. vi. 29; I Chron. iv. 26; I Chron. vi. 42; I Chron. xxiii. 7; I Chron. xxv. 17; I Chron. xxvii. 27; I Kings i. 8; I Kings iv. 18; I Chron. v. 4; II Chron. xxix. 14; II Chron. xxxi. 12; Esther ii. 5; I Chron. iii. 19; Ezra x. 23; Ezra x. 33; Ezra x. 38).

SHIMEON—a son of Harim (Ezra x. 31).

SHIMMA—a son of Jesse (I Chron. ii. 13).

SHIMON—a descendant of Caleb (I Chron. iv. 20).

SHIMRATH—a Benjamite, son of Shimhi (I Chron. viii. 21).

SHIMRI—There are four men of this name (see I Chron. iv. 37; I Chron. xi. 45; I Chron. xxvi. 10; II Chron. xxix. 13).

SHIMRON—a son of Issachar (Gen. xlvi. 13).

SHIMSHAI—a scribe in the days of Ezra (Ezra iv. 8).

SHINAB—king of Admah; defeated by Chedorlaomer (Gen. xiv. 2).

SHIPHI—a son of Allon (I Chron. iv. 37).

SHIPHTAN—father of Kemuel (Num. xxxiv. 24).

SHISHA—a scribe under Solomon (I Kings iv. 3). (Probably the same as Shavsha).

SHISHAK—a king of Egypt who sheltered Jeroboam when he was a fugitive rebel. In the fifth year of Rehoboam's reign he made an expedition against Judah, pillaging both the Temple and the King's palace and carrying away much spoil from both places (I Kings xi. 40).

SHITRAI—one of David's chief shepherds (I Chron. xxvii. 29).

SHIZA—father of Adina (I Chron. xi. 42).

SHOBAB—1. A son of Caleb (I Chron. ii. 18). 2. A son of David (II Sam. v. 14).

SHOBACH—commander-in-chief under Hadarezer (II Sam. x. 16).

SHOBAI—founder of a family of porters under Zerubbabel (Ezra ii. 42).

SHOBAL—a son of Caleb (I Chron. ii. 50).

SHOBEK—a Jewish chief with Nehemiah (Neh. x. 24).

SHOBI—a son of Nahash (II Sam. xvii. 27).

SHOHAM—a Levite, son of Merari and Jaaziah (I Chron. xxiv. 27).

SHOMER — 1. A son of

Heber (I Chron. vii. 32).
2. Mother of Jehozabad
(II Kings xii. 21).

SHUAH—1. Youngest son of
Abraham by Keturah (Gen.
xxv. 2). 2. Brother of Chelub (I Chron. iv. 11). 3. A
Canaanitess, whose daugh-
ter became Judah's wife
(Gen. xxxviii. 2).

SHUHAM—founder of the
Shuhamite family (Num.
xxvi. 42).

SHUNI—founder of the Shu-
nites (Gen. xlvi. 16).

SHUPHAM—a son of Ben-
jamin (Num. xxvi. 39).

SHUPPIM—a porter in Da-
vid's reign (I Chron. xxvi.
16).

SHUTHELAH—a son of
Ephraim (Num. xxvi. 35).

SIAHA—a family of Nethi-
nim, who returned with
Zerubbabel (Ezra. ii. 44).

SIBBECHAI—one of Da-
vid's mighty men (II Sam.
xxi. 18).

SIHON—a king of the Amo-
rites, whose capital was at
Heshbon. Slain in battle
after refusing a passage to
the Israelites through his
territory (Num. xxi. 21).

SILAS—a contraction of
SILVANUS—a distin-
guished member of the
Apostolic Church. He
accompanied Paul to An-
tioch to make known the
decision of the Church at
Jerusalem (Acts. xv. 22).
Also accompanied Paul on
his second missionary journey (Acts xvi. 19, etc.).

SIMEON—1. A son of Jacob.
He took part in a cruel
massacre at Shechem.
Afterwards on the visit of
the brethren to Egypt to
treat with Joseph he be-
came bound as surety for
the return of the rest (Gen.
xxix. 33). 2. A righteous
and devout man, who was
told by the Holy Spirit
that he should not see
death until he had seen
the Lord Christ (Luke iii.
30). 3. A Christian prophet
in the Church at Antioch,
surnamed Niger (black) and
therefore possibly of Afri-
can birth (Acts xiii. 1).

SIMON—1. Father of
Judas Iscariot (John
vi. 71). 2. A Pharisee
who invited Christ to his
house. 3. Simon the
Zealot (Matt. x. 4). 4.
A householder in Bethany
in whose house our Lord
was "anointed" (Matt.
xxvi. 6-13). 5. Simon
Peter (see " Peter "). 6.
The Cyrenian who bore
Christ's cross (Matt. xxvii.
32). 7. Better known as
Simon Magus, the sorcerer
converted through the
instrumentality of Peter
(Acts viii. 9-24). 8. Si-
mon, a tanner, with whom
Peter lodged at Joppa
(Acts ix. 43). 9. One of
our Lord's brothers (Matt.
xiii. 55).

SISAMAI—a son of Eleasah
of Judah (I Chron. ii. 40).

SISERA—commander of the
army of Jabin, king of the
Canaanites, who reigned at
Hazor. Under Deborah,
Barak headed a revolt
against Jabin, and Sisera
was slain by the treachery
of the wife of Heber the
Kenite (Judg. iv. 2).

SO—the king of Egypt, on
whom Hoshea depended

when he rebelled against Shalmaneser of Assyria, but who failed him when the time for action came (II Kings xvii. 2-6).

SODI—father of Gaddiel and spy from tribe of Zebulun (Num. xiii. 10).

SOLOMON—a son of David and Bathsheba. Was appointed by David as his successor to the throne. In a vision he chose wisdom rather than wealth and was endowed by God with both gifts, so that his name became famous throughout the world. The work of building the Temple, which his father had been forbidden to carry out, was performed under Solomon's direction, and a world-famous building resulted. His wisdom and wealth brought visitors from afar, as, for instance, the queen of Sheba. Commerce also flourished under his reign. In his old age, however, he fell into sin, sowing seeds of evil, which brought forth a plentiful crop after his death. He reigned for forty years (see II Sam. xii. 24, etc., and very many corresponding references).

S O P A T E R—a Christian from Berea who went in advance of Paul from Macedonia to Troas (Acts xx. 4).

SOSIPATER — a Christian who joined with Paul in sending salutations from Rome (Rom. xvi. 21).

SOSTHENES—a ruler of the synagogue at Corinth, who was " beaten before the judgment seat," while " Galio cared for none of these things," i.e., declined to take sides (Acts xviii. 17).

SOTAI—one of Solomon's servants (Ezra ii. 55).

STEPHANAS—Paul's first convert in Achaia. His household also became Christian (I Cor. i. 16).

STEPHEN—a shining light in the early Church. When deacons were chosen to administer alms to the needy, " they chose Stephen, a man full of faith and of the Holy Ghost." He appears to have been a man of considerable culture and of specially fine character. His success brought about an attack upon him, and after making his famous " apology " before the Sanhedrin he was stoned to death. It would appear from subsequent references that he was a vital factor in the conversion of Paul, who was present at his martyrdom (Acts vi. 5).

SUSANNA—One of the women who ministered to Jesus of their substance (Luke viii. 3).

SYNTYCHE—a somewhat quarrelsome woman in the Philippian Church (Phil. iv. 2).

T

TABEEL (or TABEAL)—1. Father of a puppet king set up in Jerusalem by

Rezin and Pekah (Isaiah vii. 6). 2. A petty Persian governor who complained to Artaxerxes Longimanus about the rebuilding of the wall of Jerusalem (Ezra iv. 7).

TABITHA—Aramaic form of Dorcas (which *see*).

TABRIMON—father of Benhadad I of Syria (I Kings xv. 18).

TAHAN—an Ephraimite, son of Telah (I Chron. vii. 25).

TAHPENES—a queen of Egypt at the time Hadad ; came as a fugitive from Solomon (I Kings xi. 19).

TALMAI—1. A descendant of Anak; slain by Caleb (Joshua xv. 14). 2. A king of Geshur whose daughter became one of David's wives (II Sam. iii. 3).

TALMON—a porter (I Chron. ix. 17).

TAMAR—1. Wife of Er, son of Judah (Gen. xxxviii. 6). 2. A beautiful sister of Absalom (I Chron. iii 9). 3. A daughter of Absalom (II Sam. xiv. 27).

TAMMUZ—a Syrian divinity corresponding to the Roman Adonis (Ezek. viii. 14).

TANHUMETH—a Netophathite, who came to Gedaliah (II Kings xxv. 23).

TAPHATH — daughter of Solomon and wife of Abinadab (I Kings iv. 11).

TAPPUAH—a son of Hebron (I Chron. ii. 43).

TAREA—a son of Micah (I Chron. viii. 35).

TARSHISH—three men of this name are mentioned (*see* Gen. x. 4 ; I Chron. vii. 10 ; Esther i. 14).

TATNAI—a Persian governor of part of Palestine (Ezra v. 3).

TEBAH—a son of Nahor (Gen. xxii. 24).

TEBALIAH—a Merarite Levite (I Chron. xxvi. 11).

TEHINNAH—a man of Judah (I Chron. iv. 12).

TELAH—a descendant of Ephraim (I Chron. vii. 25).

TELEM—a porter under Ezra (Ezra x. 24).

TEMA—ninth son of Ishmael (Gen. xxv. 15).

TEMAN—son of Eliphaz and grandson of Esau (Gen. xxxvi. 11).

TEMENI—a son of Ashur (I Chron. iv. 6).

TERAH—son of Nahor and father of Abraham ; seems to have been an idolater and even a maker of idols. Abraham accompanied him to Haran, where they dwelt till Terah's death (Gen. xi. 24-32).

TERESH—a chamberlain under King Ahasuerus, whose murder he plotted, for which design he was executed (Esther ii. 21).

TERTIUS—Paul's secretary; at Paul's dictation he wrote the Epistle to the *Romans* (Rom. xvi. 22).

TERTULLUS — a Roman orator or advocate who appeared against Paul before Felix (Acts xxiv. 1-8).

THADDÆUS—surname of Lebbæus (Matt. x. 3).

THAHASH—son of Nahor (Gen. xxii. 24).

THEOPHILUS—the unknown Christian to whom Luke addressed both his

Gospel and *The Acts* (Luke i. 3 and Acts i. 1).

THEUDAS—a rebel mentioned in Acts v. 36.

THOMAS—one of Christ's twelve Apostles. His chief characteristic seems to have been a certain hesitancy of belief without what he considered adequate proof. He appears to have been intensely loyal to Christ. He was with the rest in the upper room after the Ascension. Tradition suggests that he went as an evangelist to Persia, where he died, though other places also claim to have been the place of his decease (*see* Matt. x. 3, etc.).

TIBERIUS CÆSAR—son of Tiberius Claudius Nero; an evil ruler of chief concern here, because in his " fifteenth year " John the Baptist began to preach (Luke iii. 1).

TIBNI—a son of Ginath; he sought the throne of Israel, but was slain by Omri (I Kings xvi. 21).

TIDAL—" king of Goiim " (i.e. " king of the nations ") (Genesis xiv. 1).

TIGLATH-PILESER—a king of Assyria, whom Ahaz called to his aid against Rezin and Pekah. Ahaz lived to regret the alliance (II Kings. xvi. 10).

TIKVAH—father-in-law of Huldah the prophetess (II Kings xxii. 14).

TILON—a son of Shimon, of the tribe of Judah (I Chron. iv. 20).

TIMÆUS—the father of Bartimæus (Mark x. 46).

TIMNA—a concubine of Eliphaz, Esau's eldest son, and mother of Amalek (Gen. xxxvi. 12).

TIMNAH—a duke of Edom (Gen. xxxvi. 40).

TIMON—one of the original seven deacons of Acts vi. 5.

TIMOTHY (also called TIMOTHEUS)—a Christian convert, first met by Paul on his second missionary journey at Derbe or Lystra, probably the latter. Became closely associated with Paul in the work of the Gospel. Paul appears to have held him in affectionate regard, as is testified by the tone and contents of I and II *Timothy* Epistles (*see* Acts xvi. 1) and the companion references, as well as the two Epistles named.

TIRAS—youngest son of Japheth (Gen. x. 2).

TIRHAKAH—a king of Ethiopia, who came to fight with Sennacherib in the campaign against Hezekiah (II Kings xix. 9).

TIRHANAH—a son of Caleb (I Chron. ii. 48).

TIRSHATHA—the Persian title given to the ruler of Judah. Zerubbabel was so called (Ezra ii. 63).

TIRZAH — the youngest among the five daughters of Zelophehad (Num. xxvi. 33).

TITUS—a Christian evangelist of Greek descent, who became a companion of Paul and who was associated with that leader in much subsequent evangelization. Paul sent him to labour in Crete, and the last mention we have of him says that he went to Dalmatia (Gal. ii. 3-5) (*see* also the Epistle which bears his name).

TOAH—a Kohathite Levite (I Chron. vi. 34).

TOBIAH — 1. The founder of a family in Ezra's time (Ezra ii. 60). 2. An Ammonite servant who poured ridicule upon the Jews' effort to rebuild the wall of Jerusalem (Neh. ii. 10).

TOBIJAH — 1. One of the Levites sent by Jehoshaphat to teach the cities of Judah (II Chron. xvii. 8). 2. A Jew of the captivity (Zech. vi. 10).

TOGARMAH—youngest son of Gomer (Gen. x. 3).

TOHU—a son of Zuph, belonging to Mount Ephraim (I Sam. i. 1).

TOLA—1. Eldest son of Issachar (Gen. xlvi. 13). 2. An Israelite " judge " whose judgeship lasted twenty-three years (Judg. x. 1).

TROPHIMUS — a Gentile Christian of Ephesus, who was with Paul for a time (Acts xxi. 29).

TRYPHENA—a woman of Rome, whose name is coupled with Tryphosa, to whom Paul sent his salutations (Rom. xvi. 12).

TRYPHOSA—a woman of Rome, whose name is coupled with Tryphena, to whom Paul sent his salutations (Rom. xvi. 12).

TUBAL—fifth son of Japheth (Gen. x. 2).

TUBAL-CAIN—a son of Lamech, he was " the forger of every cutting instrument in brass and in iron " (Gen. iv. 22).

TYCHICUS—an Asiatic Christian associated with Paul (Acts xx. 4).

TYRANNUS—an Ephesian in whose school Paul " disputed " with a view to making Christianity better known, when he had no longer access to the Jewish synagogue (Acts xix. 9).

U

UEL—a son of Bani (Ezra x. 34).

ULAM—a Manassite, son of Sheresh (I Chron. vii. 16).

ULLA—an Asherite, father of Arah (I Chron. vii. 39).

UNNI — 1. A Levite, who acted as porter in David's reign (I Chron. xv. 18). 2. A Levite in the time of Zerubbabel (Neh. xii. 9).

URBANE—A Christian to whom Paul sent his salutations (Rom. xvi. 9).

URIAH—1. A Hittite whom David had placed in the forefront of the battle that he might be slain, and so not know of an intrigue with his wife on the part of his sovereign (II Sam. xi. 39). 2. A priest in the days of Isaiah, probably the same as Urijah (Isaiah viii. 2). 3. A priest in Ezra's time (Ezra viii. 33).

URIEL—1. A Kohathite Levite in the days of David (I Chron. vi. 24). 2. A man of Gibeah, grandfather of Abijah (II Chron. xiii. 2).

URIJAH—1. The high

priest of Ahaz's reign, whom Ahaz asked to make an altar which was to be a copy of one seen by the king at Damascus (II Kings xvi. 10).   2. A prophet, son of Shemaiah of Kirjath-jearim, who fled for his life to Egypt from the wrath of King Jehoiakim (Jer. xxvi. 20).

UTHAI—1. A son of Ammihud (I Chron. ix. 4).   2. A son of Bigvai (Ezra viii. 14).

UZ—1. Grandson of Shem (Gen. x. 23).   2. Eldest son of Dishan (Gen. xxxvi. 28).   3. Eldest son of Nahor and Milcah (Gen. xxii. 21). *Variant*, Huz.

UZAI—father of Palal, who helped to rebuild the wall of Jerusalem (Neh. iii. 25).

UZAL—sixth son of Joktan (Gen. x. 27).

UZZA—1. Son of Merari (I Chron. vi. 29).   2. A Benjamite, descendant of Ehud (I Chron. viii. 7). 3. Founder of a family of Nethinim, who returned with Ezra (Ezra ii. 49).

UZZAH—a son of Abinadab; struck dead for touching the Ark (II Sam. vi. 3).

UZZI—there are six men of this name, none of whom is important, mentioned in the following references : I Chron. vii. 2 ; I Chron. vi. 5 ; I Chron. vii. 7 ; I Chron. ix. 8 ; Neh. xi. 22 ; Neh. xii. 42 ; Neh. xii. 19.

UZZIA—an Asherite, one of David's mighty men (I Chron. xi. 44).

UZZIAH — 1. A Kohathite Levite, son of Shaul (I Chron. vi. 24).   2. The father of Jehonathan, in David's time (I Chron. xxvii. 25).   3. A king of Judah, also known as Azariah.   He succeeded his father Amaziah and ascended the throne when he was about 16. He worshipped Jehovah, but did not remove the "high places" in his realm.   He gained important victories over the Philistines, the Arabs, the Ammonites, etc. He wrought improvements in Jerusalem and established his realm in many ways.   Elated by his prosperity, he entered the Temple against the remonstrances of the priests and was struck with leprosy, from which he never recovered.   He reigned for 52 years.   Isaiah tells us concerning himself, that it was "in the year that King Uzziah died that he saw the Lord," and thus started on his great prophetic work (II Kings xv. 1; etc.):   4. A priest, son of Harim (Ezra x. 21).   5. The son of a certain Zechariah (Neh. xi. 4).

UZZIEL—1. A Levite youngest son of Kohath and uncle of Aaron (Ex. vi, 18). 2. A Benjamite, son of Bela (I Chron. vii. 7). 3. An instrumentalist in David's reign (I Chron. xxv. 4).   4. A Levite, son of Jeduthun (II Chron. xxix. 14).   5. A Simeonite captain in Hezekiah's reign. He led a successful expedition against the Amalekites (I Chron. iv. 42).   6. A goldsmith who helped to build the wall of Jerusalem (Neh. iii. 8).

V

VAJEZATHA—youngest son of Haman (Esther ix. 9).

VANIAH—son of Bani (Ezra x. 36).

VASHTI—the queen of the Persian sovereign Ahasuerus (? Xerxes). With maidenly modesty she refused to have her beauty exploited before the king's guests, and was in consequence deposed in favour of Esther (Esther i. 9 ff.).

VOPHSI—father of Nahbi the Naphtali spy (Num. xiii. 14).

Z

ZAAVAN (equivalent, ZAVAN)—a son of Ezer, descendant of Ephraim (Gen. xxxvi. 27).

ZABAD—1. A descendant of Ephraim (I Chron. vii. 21). 2. One of David's mighty men (I Chron. xi. 41). 3. The name also occurs in II Chron. xxiv. 26 ; Ezra x. 27 ; Ezra x. 33 ; Ezra x. 43.

ZABBAI—a son of Bebai (Neh. iii. 20).

ZABBUD—a follower of Ezra (Ezra viii. 14).

ZABDI—four men of this name are mentioned. See Josh. vii. 1 ; I Chron. viii 19 ; I Chron. xxvii. 27 ; Neh. xi. 17.

ZABDIEL — 1. Father of Jashobeam (I Chron. xxvii 2). 2. Son of Haggedolim (Neh. xi. 14).

ZABUD—a priest, son of Nathan (I Kings iv. 5).

ZACCAI—founder of a family which accompanied Zerubbabel (Ezra ii. 9).

ZACCHÆUS—a rich publican, short of stature, who sought to see Jesus, and was surprised when Jesus spent some time at his house. He agreed to restore fourfold anything he had wrongfully taken, and was rewarded by Christ saying : "This day is salvation come to this house," etc. (Luke xix. 1-10).

ZACCUR (also called ZACCHUR)—seven men of this name are mentioned in the following passages : Num. xiii. 4 ; I Chron. iv. 26 ; I Chron. xxiv. 27 ; I. Chron. xxv. 2, 10 ; Neh. iii. 2 ; Neh. x. 12 ; Neh. xiii. 13.

ZACHARIAH—1. See II Kings xv. 8 ; 2. See II Kings xviii. 2 ; 3. A son of Barachaias, slain by the Jews, " between the sanctuary and the altar." He wrote the Old Testament book which bears his name. Some doubt is cast upon this, however, and the above reference may be connected with Zachariah the son of Jehoida (II Chron. xxiv. 20). 4. Father of John the Baptist (Luke i. 5, etc.), known, however, by the Greek form Zacharias (see Zechariah.)

ZADOK—a descendant of Eleazar the son of Aaron. Well known in David's reign, when he was joint high priest with Abiathar ;

assisted in the anointing of Solomon (II Sam. viii. 17). Five more men of this name are mentioned in Scripture. *See* I Chron. vi. 12; II Kings xv. 33; Neh. iii. 4; Neh. iii. 29; I Chron. ix. II.

ZAHAM—a son of Rehoboam (II Chron. xi. 19).

ZALAPH—father of Hanun (Neh. iii. 30).

ZALMON—one of David's mighty men (II Sam. xxiii. 28).

ZALMUNNA—one of the two kings of Midian slain by Gideon (Judg. viii. 5).

ZAPHNATH-PAANEAH— the Egyptian name given to Joseph by Pharaoh (Gen. xli. 45).

ZARAH—*see* Zerah.

ZATTHU—a chief of the people who sealed the covenant (Neh. x. 14).

ZAZA—a man of the tribe of Judah (I Chron. ii. 33).

ZEBADIAH—Nine men of this name are mentioned. *See* I Chron. viii. 15; I Chron. viii. 17; I Chron. xii. 7; I Chron. xxvii. 7; I Chron. xxvi. 1; II Chron. xvii. 8; II Chron. xix. 11; Ezra viii. 8; Ezra x. 20.

ZEBAH—one of the kings of Midian (Judg. viii. 10).

ZEBEDEE—husband of Salome and father of James and John (Matt. iv. 21, 22).

ZEBINA—a son of Nebo (Ezra x. 43).

ZEBUDAH—mother of King Jehoiakim (II Kings xxiii. 36).

ZEBUL—governor of Shechem (Judg. ix. 28).

ZEBULUN—tenth son of Jacob (Gen. xxx. 20).

ZECHARIAH (*Variant*, Zachariah (which *see*)–twenty -nine men of this name are mentioned (*see* I Chron. ix. 37; I Chron. xxvi. 2; I Chron. xv. 18; I Chron. xv. 24; I Chron. xxiv. 25; I Chron. xxvi. II; I Chron. xxvii. 21; II Chron. xx. 14; II Chron. xvii. 7; II Chron. xxi. 2; II Chron. xxiv. 20; II Chron. xxvi. 5; II Kings xiv. 29; I Chron. v. 7; Isaiah viii. 2; II Kings xviii. 2.; II Chron. xxix. 13; II Chron. xxxiv. 12; II Chron. xxxv. 8; Neh. xi 5; Neh. xi. 12; the Prophet: Zech. i. I; Neh. xi. 4; Ezra viii. 3; Ezra viii. II; Neh. viii. 4; Ezra x. 26; Neh. xii. 35; Neh. xii. 16).

ZEDEKIAH — 1. Son of Chenaanah (I Kings xxii. 24). 2. Son of Hananiah (Jer. xxxvi. 12). 3. A lying prophet (Jer. xxix. 21). 4. Nebuchadnezzar's name for Mattaniah, one of Jehoiakim's sons, whom he appointed as vassal king of Judah (II Kings xxiv. 17) (*see* Mattaniah). 5. A Jewish dignitary, also called Zidkijah (Neh. x. 1).

ZEEB—a Midianitish prince put to death by Gideon (Judg. vii. 25).

ZELEK—an Ammonite, one of David's mighty men (II Sam. xxiii. 37).

ZELOPHEHAD—a Manassite, son of Hepher (Num. xxvi. 33).

ZEMIRA—a Benjamite (I Chron. vii. 8).

ZENAS—a lawyer mentioned

by Titus (*equivalent*, Zenodorus) (Titus iii. 13).

ZEPHANIAH—1. A Kohathite Levite (I Chron. vi. 36). 2. A prophet (Zeph. i. 1). 3. A priest, son of Maaseiah (Jer. xxi. 1). 4. Father of Josiah (Zech. vi. 10).

ZEPHO—a son of Eliphaz (Gen. xxxvi. 11).

ZEPHON—eldest son of Gad (Num. xxvi. 15).

ZERAH (*equivalent*, ZARAH) —there are five men of this name mentioned in Scripture (*see* Gen. xxxvi. 13; Gen. xxxviii. 30; Num. xxvi. 13; I Chron. vi. 21; II Chron. xiv. 9).

ZERAHIAH—1. A priest (Ezra vii. 4). 2. Father of Elihoenai (Ezra viii. 4).

ZERESH—wife of Haman (Esther vi. 13).

ZERETH—son of Ashur (I Chron. iv. 7).

ZEROR—son of Bechorath (I Sam. ix. 1).

ZERUAH—mother of Jeroboam (II Kings xi. 26).

ZERUBBABEL—son of Pedaiah (often called " son of Shealtiel ") appointed by Cyrus (as lineal descendant of the old Jewish kings) Persian governor of Judah. He was leader of the people in the great work of rebuilding the Temple, though he met with much hindrance and opposition (Haggai ii. 21).

ZERUIAH—sister of King David (I Sam. xxvi. 6).

ZETHAM—a Gershonite Levite (I Chron. xxiii. 8).

ZETHAN—a Benjamite, son of Bilhan (I Chron. vii. 10).

ZETHAR—a chamberlain at the court of Ahasuerus (Esther i. 10).

ZIA—a Gadite (I Chron. v. 13).

ZIBA—a slave of Saul's house; was instrumental in gaining recognition for little Mephibosheth at David's court (II Sam. ix. 1-13).

ZIBEON—a Hivite (Gen. xxxvi. 2).

ZIBIA—a Benjamite (I Chron. viii. 9).

ZIBIAH—a woman of Beersheba, wife of Jehoash, king of Judah (II Kings xii. 1).

ZICHRI—twelve men of this name are mentioned in Scripture, as follows: Ex. vi. 21; 1 Chron. viii. 19; I Chron. viii. 23; I Chron. viii. 27; I Chron. ix. 15; I Chron. xxvi. 25 ;. I Chron. xxvii. 16; II Chron. xvii. 16; II Chron. xxiii. 1; xxvii. 16; II Chron. xvii. 16; II Chron. xxiii. 1; II Chron. xxviii. 7; Neh. xi. 9; Neh. xii. 17.

ZIHA—founder of a family of Nethinim (Ezra ii. 43).

ZILLAH—one of Lamech's wives; mother of Tubal-cain (Gen. iv. 19).

ZILPAH—maid servant of Leah (Gen. xxix. 24).

ZILTHAI—1. Son of Shimhi (I Chron. viii. 20); 2. A Manassite (I Chron. xii. 20).

ZIMMAH—1. A Gershonite Levite (I Chron. vi. 20). 2. Father of Joah (II Chron. xxix. 12).

ZIMRAN—eldest son of Abraham (Gen. xxv. 2).

ZIMRI—a military officer who assassinated Elah, king of Israel, and wiped out

Baasha's house. He assumed kingship, but when Omri marched against him, Zimri burnt his capital and perished in the flames (I Kings xvi. 9). For others of this name *see :* I Chron. ii. 6 ; Num. xxv. 14 ; I Chron. viii. 36.

ZIPH—son of Jehaleleel (I Chron. iv. 16).

ZIPPOR—father of Balak king of Moab (Num. xxii. 2).

ZIPPORAH—a daughter of "the Priest of Midian," who became wife of Moses (Ex. ii. 21).

ZITHRI—a Levite, youngest son of Uzziel (Ex. vi. 22).

ZIZA — 1. Son of Shiphi (I Chron. iv. 37). 2. Son of Rehoboam (II Chron. xi. 20).

ZOBEBAH—son of Hakkas (I Chron. iv. 8).

ZOHAR—1. Father of Ephron (Gen. xxiii. 8). 2. Fifth son of Simeon (Gen. xlvi. 10).

ZOHETH—a son of Ishi (I Chron. iv. 20).

ZOPHAH—eldest son of Helem (I Chron. vii. 35).

ZOPHAI—son of Elkanah (I Chron. vi. 26).

ZOPHAR—one of Job's "friends." (Job ii. 11).

ZUAR—father of Nethaneel of Issachar (Num. i. 8).

ZUPH—ancestor of the prophet Samuel (I Chron. vi. 35).

ZUR—1. A Midianite chief or king (Num. xxv. 15). 2. Father of Kish, Saul's father (I Chron. viii. 30).

ZURIEL—a leading Merarite Levite in the wilderness (Num. iii. 35).

ZURISHADDAI—father of Shelumiel ; the latter was prince of the Simeonites in the wilderness (Num. i. 6).